ASK ME WHY

based on the Yorkshire Television programme *Don't Ask Me*

Geoffrey Hoyle and Janice Robertson

ASK ME WHY

illustrated by Rowan Barnes Murphy

based on the Yorkshire Television programme *Don't Ask Me*

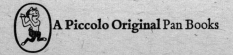 A Piccolo Original Pan Books

First published 1976 by Pan Books Ltd,
Cavaye Place, London SW10 9PG
2nd printing 1977
© Trident Television Ltd 1976
ISBN 0 330 24822 7
Printed in Great Britain by
Richard Clay (The Chaucer Press) Ltd, Bungay, Suffolk

For three years now, Yorkshire Television have been running a popular science question-and-answer series, *Don't Ask Me*. The programmes were prompted by questions sent in by viewers, but Yorkshire Television have received many more than their experts could deal with in the shows. So we have answered some of the extra ones in this book, and, to remind you of what fun science can be, included also a few of the more fascinating theories advanced on the air by their star experts Magnus Pyke, Miriam Stoppard and David Bellamy.

G.H.
J.R.

Why don't penguins get frostbitten feet?

When we touch ice in the refrigerator, our fingers often stick and burn. This is because we sweat through the skin of our hands (and feet), and the thin layer of salty water freezes instantly on contact with something very cold. This doesn't happen to the penguin as it has no sweat glands on its feet, and there are other devices that help it as well. The blood in the arteries is cooled as it runs down to the feet because the arteries are placed very close to the veins; the cold blood returning to its heart takes heat from these arteries to save on overall heat loss.

Watch a penguin closely as it stands. It may have arched its feet to rest only on heels and toe, or it may have rocked right back so that its tail feathers support it, leaving the eggs nestling on its forefeet snug and dry. On the soles of its feet it has little bumpy pads called *papillae* and only these small areas touch the ground.

The penguin's body is wonderfully designed for Antarctic conditions: compact and round, with a dense plumage and a layer of insulating fat two to three centimetres (0·8–1·2 inches) thick.

But what about those penguins that live on islands off South America and South Africa? They are cleverly adapted for the heat as well. Under the flippers are very few feathers but lots of blood vessels, so the penguin can lose heat quickly simply by flapping its wings.

Why do camels have humps?

No, it is not to store water as many people think. It does help the camel to spend long periods in the desert, though, because the hump is where the camel stores fat.

Most other animals, including man, carry fatty layers fairly evenly distributed under the skin. This is fine in a cold or temperate climate, but in high temperatures such animals are too well insulated and quickly become dangerously hot.

In any case, the camel does not need to be so cool. Its 'normal' temperature can be anything between 34° and 41° centigrade (93° and 105° Fahrenheit). So while man, striving to maintain a body temperature of around 37° centigrade (98·4° Fahrenheit) may lose in sweat as much as a litre (nearly two pints) of water in a single hour, the camel, making a much smaller adjustment, will sweat far less.

And the camel's blood cells are specially adapted for the conditions it has to face. When the camel driver is short of water, his blood becomes dense and thick. His heart can hardly pump it round, let alone circulate it to the skin so that heat can dissipate. The camel's red blood cells are thicker-walled and oval-shaped and, far from letting precious water go, they draw it from other body fluids by osmosis.

During the day the camel's hair lies flat against its skin, but in the cold desert night it rises up to make a thick layer of luxury insulation. The driver huddles up close on the leeward side. When at last they reach an oasis, the camel may have travelled for two weeks without a drink. It gulps down as much as 112 litres (twenty-five gallons) of water, plumping out all its tissues and firming up its hump.

Why do skunks stink?

The skunk, also called the 'polecat' or the 'zorrino', is a carnivore of the weasel family and is only found in the New World. The offensive smell is produced by glands on either side of its anus.

The odour is so powerful that it can be smelled half a mile away.

The skunk uses it to define its own territory and to warn off enemies. But it may try other means to deter the enemy first. It may stamp its feet, or the spotted skunk, *Spilogale*, will handstand on its front legs. Only if the threat continues or increases will it turn its hindquarters towards the target and eject a fine spray of yellow stinking liquid as far as four metres (twelve feet).

Species of skunk vary in size, but the common skunk *Mephitis mephitica* is about as big as a heavy cat. It has black fur with a streak of white on the back and a long bushy tail. Most species are nocturnal. They live on the ground and feed mainly on rodents, frogs, insects' eggs and occasionally poultry.

Skunks can be deodorized if their stink glands are removed, and they make interesting pets. Their pelts are used commercially and are often plucked and dyed to simulate more precious skins. Even their 'scent' gland secretions have a value: as a base for perfumes!

Why do lemmings throw themselves off cliffs?

They don't. But they do make periodic mass migrations. Their normal home is in the mountains of Scandinavia, but they are very prolific breeders and from time to time over-population forces great rivers of them to descend. They can only travel downhill, though they sometimes go several miles each day. When they come to water they are reluctant to swim but if there is no alternative they will try. And they do often drown if the water is at all rough. Then hundreds of dead bodies are washed up on the shores of Norwegian fjords, giving rise to the great lemming myth.

Why do pearls form in oysters?

Oyster shells are lined with mother-of-pearl, the same material as the pearl itself. When some foreign particle – perhaps a grain of sand – gets lodged inside the oyster's protective mantle, the oyster covers it with layers of shell material to prevent it harming the mollusc's soft interior. If there is no deforming pressure, the pearl will grow into a perfect sphere or pear shape. But cysts lodged in the strong muscle tissue cannot resist the pressure of the tough fibres; they develop irregularly and are known as 'baroque' pearls. Others that form between the shell and the mantle grow into a hemisphere called a 'blister' pearl, that is flat on one side.

Pearls can be produced artificially by inserting a tiny piece of grit inside the oyster's shell. These are known as cultivated pearls, and are still essentially genuine. Some artificial pearls are built up from layers of synthetic material almost like the natural growth; but others are simply painted beads.

The giant clam of the Philippines produces very large pearls. The heaviest recorded weighed just over 6·5 kilogrammes (about fourteen pounds). But the best natural pearls are found in the Persian Gulf, in the waters around Ceylon and off the north-east coast of Borneo. The oysters are collected by divers who work without modern breathing equipment and go down to depths of between fifteen and thirty-six metres (fifty and 120 feet). Some can stay on the sea-bed for as long as six minutes – but fifty to eighty seconds is the average for a dive.

How do pigeons find their way home?

Within about thirty kilometres (twenty miles) of their loft, they are guided by familiar landmarks; but if they are released a hundred kilometres (sixty miles) or more from home, they seem to navigate by the sun. Set free within thirty and a hundred kilometres from their base, the pigeons scatter in all directions and have difficulty finding their way; and the same is true if the day is overcast.

But if the pigeon is guided by the sun, it must somehow correct its 'compass' to allow for the sun's movement east to west across the sky. It must have some sort of 'clock' inside its head to know where the sun should be at certain times of day.

Thinking this, a group of scientists decided to keep birds in artificial conditions. The pigeons' 'days' and 'nights' were shifted so that though they still experienced a light/dark cycle, the timing was different: they were out of phase with the world outside. After four days their 'clocks' were six hours slow, and they were accepting a 'day' that lasted from noon till midnight. When these birds were released at noon, they saw the sun in a six a.m. position and flew off at right angles to their correct home bearing.

But the pigeons could only recognize a difference in the height of the sun's path to an accuracy of $\frac{3}{4}°$. This represents a change of latitude equal to a distance of a hundred kilometres, and explains why the birds have difficulty on journeys of less than that unless they recognize landmarks. Beyond a hundred kilometres, they use the path of the sun. If at a given time it is lower at the release point than it would be at home, the pigeons fly south; if it is higher they go north. For east/west orientation, scientists believe that the birds' 'clock' mechanism enables them to recall the position of the sun above their loft at any given time. They can then compare this with what they see when they are set free.

The pigeon's eye is particularly well-adapted for looking at the sun. The light-sensitive retina is covered with coloured oil-droplets that reduce glare. It is almost as if it has a pair of built-in sunglasses.

How does a salmon find its way back to the same river to spawn?

Salmon certainly do seem to return, if not always to the same river, at least to the area in which they hatched. They probably do this partly by sight, for fish are able to orientate by the sun to steer a particular course. But this cannot be the whole answer. The young smolt drifts passively down to the sea in the shallower water near the bank, while the mature salmon that returns perhaps three years later swims strenuously against the current in the deep middle waters. Any landmarks from its earlier journey would be beyond its visual range.

But the salmon's sense organs can detect very small differences in the chemical characteristics of the water in different streams and ocean currents. Probably saltiness, acidity, temperature, dissolved gases and turbulence all play their part; and the salmon may also recognize the general nature of the water-bed, the sound of rapids and the types of food available as it finds its way home to spawn.

Is it true that eels from all over the world breed in one place?

Yes it is. All European and North American eels (*Anguilla anguilla* and *Anguilla rostrata*) spawn in the warm waters of the Atlantic, at depths of about 400 to 700 metres (1,300 to 2,300 feet) in an area called the Sargasso Sea.

The eel goes through several different forms in its life cycle, which is rather like the salmon's in reverse. At first the eggs develop into 'leptocephali' – transparent leaf-like forms with relatively small heads that are carried by the Gulf Stream to the shallow waters of the continental shelves. When they are about two and a half years old and about eight centimetres (three inches) long, a metamorphosis occurs. The leptocephali are transformed into elvers, which are bottom-dwelling and cylindrical in form. They arrive in coastal waters as 'glass eels' and begin to swim up freshwater streams, gathering in millions and forming a dense mass, sometimes several miles long. In fresh water they grow to full size, become yellow eels and live there for ten to fifteen years before finally changing to silver eels with enlarged eyes. These swim downstream to the sea again, return to the Sargasso Sea, spawn, and die.

What is a jelly-fish?

'Jelly-fish' is the common name for an invertebrate marine animal that has a translucent gelatinous body. They occur in all oceans but are most common in the warm tropical seas. About two hundred species are known, varying in size from fifteen millimetres (0·6 of an inch) to about 2·3 metres (seven feet) in diameter. The largest found in British waters is the rare 'Lion's mane' jelly-fish, *Cyanea capillata*, which is also known as the common sea blubber. One specimen measured at St Andrews Marine Laboratory in Fife had a body diameter of over seventy-five centimetres (thirty inches) and tentacles that stretched over 13·5 metres (forty-five feet).

The bodies of jelly-fish are about 99 per cent water, so when they are washed on to dry land they die very quickly as the body-water evaporates. But, barring accidents, the normal life span is one to three months, with some species surviving for about a year.

Beneath the bell- or umbrella-shaped body hangs a more or less tubular projection, the 'manubrium' or 'proboscis', with the mouth at the free end. Radial canals, usually four in number or some multiple of four, extend from the four-chambered stomach to the bell margin where they connect with a circular ring canal. This canal system provides for food distribution to peripheral parts of the body.

The upper surface of the bell is armed with 'nematocysts', or stinging cells, and so are the tentacles hanging from the edge of the bell. At the base of the tentacles are light-sensitive organs ('ocelli' or eyespots), balance organs ('statocysts') and other sensory organs. A system of muscles on the lower edge of the bell provides propulsion for slow movement through the water.

Jelly-fish feed on various animals that come close enough to be stung and paralysed by the nematocysts. The most venomous are the 'box jellies' of the genera *Chiropsalmus* and *Chironey* which live in the Indo-Pacific regions, for they carry a neurotoxic venom as strong as that found in the Asiatic cobra, and have caused the deaths of at least sixty people off the coast of Queensland, Australia, in the past twenty-five years. Victims die in one to three minutes. A bizarre but effective defence against them is to wear ladies' tights, and outsize versions of these are now displayed by Queensland lifesavers on surfing beaches!

What is a sea-horse?

It is a small fish of the genus *Hippocampus* in the pipefish family.
It has an elongated snout and a prehensile tail and is in fact the
only fish that can use its tail for holding on. Sea-horses are poor
swimmers and move partly by waving the fin on their back and
partly by drifting with currents. The female injects her eggs into a
pouch under the male's tail. When they hatch it seems as if the
father is giving birth.

Sea-horses are very attractive. They really do look like little
horses between five and thirty centimetres (two and twelve inches)
long. There are also certain Australian kinds which have long bony
outgrowths with flaps of skin that look very like seaweed. These
are called Leafy Sea Dragons.

Why do humming-birds hum?

Humming-birds need – and use – an enormous amount of energy
which they obtain largely by sucking nectar from flowers. While
the bird hovers on its powerful long wings, its long tubular tongue
is thrust into the blossom. The wings are moved not up and down
but almost horizontally with very rapid beats, and it is this which
makes the characteristic humming sound.

At other times, humming-birds make quick darting flights and
perform wonderful acrobatics in the air as they catch the tiny
insects which are also part of their diet.

Humming-birds live only in the New World and the West Indies,
though some migrate to Canada in the summer. They are usually
very small; the largest twenty centimetres (eight inches) long and
the smallest not much bigger than a bumblebee.

Why do cats purr?

It is probably a homing device, but no one is sure. When kittens
are born their eyes are closed, their ears undeveloped, and they
have no sense of smell. But purring can be felt as a vibration and
calls them close to their mother to feed. She often stops purring
when they begin to suck.

Purring is a low continuous rattling hum. It has nothing to do with the true voice of the cat; the vibration frequency is far lower than the sound its vocal cords produce. It is probably caused by a peculiar relaxed position of the diaphragm.

Humans tend to interpret purring as a sign of pleasure or contentment. But cats will purr in extremes of both pain and pleasure. A veterinary surgeon has reported a cat purring on the operating table as he worked.

Why doesn't the cuckoo make its own nest?

Perhaps it is too lazy. In any case, the cuckoo's parasitic habit works very well. In about mid-April, when the adult birds arrive in Britain from Africa, the males immediately start to make the characteristic 'cuckoo' noise; but the female's call is quite different, a kind of bubbling sound. She is polyandrous – that is, she will mate with several different cocks; and she makes her eggs look like those of other birds nesting nearby. She lays only one in each alien nest, and though it is usually slightly bigger, the camouflage is effective enough for the foster parents not to recognize the stranger and cast it out.

When the cuckoo chick hatches, it soon tips the rightful occupants out, working its way under the egg or chick and lifting it to the edge of the nest in a convenient hollow in its back. As a result the cuckoo gets the foster parents' undivided attention; they have to work very hard to satisfy its huge appetite. Sometimes the difference in size is so great that they have to stand on the fledgling's back to reach its mouth.

There are other species of cuckoo besides the familiar British one. The Indian Koël is also named for the noise it makes, while the Plantain Eaters, Rouracos, of tropical Africa, are sometimes as much as a metre (three feet) long and have green and blue plumage, crests on their heads and long tails. The American Cuckoo and the Grand Cuckoos, or Coucals, of Africa, India and Australia are not parasitic: they make their own nests.

Why do animals migrate?

No one is quite sure why, but the movement to and fro is always connected with the creature's breeding cycle or with the availability of food. For example, turtles, which live most of the year in the sea, must come to land to lay their eggs on the beach; but they return to the safer water as soon as they can. In mountainous country, animals come down to the valleys for winter grazing and then go back to raise their young in the seclusion of the hills; and many birds breed in the north and fly south for the winter.

The swallow breeds in Britain but winters in South Africa. The tiny ruby-throated humming-bird flies the Gulf of Mexico: eight hundred kilometres (five hundred miles) non-stop. Many of the starlings that spend their winters in Britain were hatched in Russia and will return there to breed, though some are permanent residents and do not migrate. The North American Golden Plover breeds in the Canadian Arctic, then, when the young birds are mature, flies direct from Nova Scotia to the coasts of South America across three thousand two hundred kilometres (two thousand miles) of Atlantic, or – if it comes from the Pacific coast – from Alaska to a wintering ground in Hawaii even farther away.

Although some butterflies winter in northern Europe, there are always new arrivals in the spring from the south. Darwin once saw a cloud of immigrating Large and Small Whites that looked, he said, as if it were 'snowing butterflies'. Painted Ladies and Red Admirals cannot survive a northern winter. Great crowds of them hatch in the Atlas mountains in North Africa in March, reach the Mediterranean coast in April and arrive in Britain in May and June. Individuals fly to northern Scotland and even to the Arctic Circle, a journey of over sixteen hundred kilometres (a thousand miles). But strictly speaking, the butterflies are emigrating rather than migrating, as they die in the north when the weather turns cold, rather than returning to Africa.

However, North America has a butterfly that really migrates. The huge, reddish-brown Monarchs, or Milkweeds, congregate like swallows in the autumn and gradually move south in their tens of thousands, a crowd so vast that they change the colour of foliage when they settle at night. When they reach warmer areas the Monarchs cluster on the limbs of trees for the winter, and in spring set off north again.

How do animals hibernate?

Their body temperature drops dramatically so that far less energy is required to keep the animal alive. Respiration falls, too, to only a few breaths a minute. To do this safely, the animal needs a secure burrow, nest or den, for it is quite defenceless in this torpid state.

The hibernating creature lives mainly on a thick layer of stored fat, but every few weeks, usually when the weather becomes a little warmer, many animals wake. The body temperature rises and after an hour or so the animal starts to move about. Rodents then feed from stores of food hidden away the previous autumn. The dormouse, however, grows so fat at harvest time that he can scarcely move. He curls into a ball with his forepaws against his cheeks and his tail wrapped round his head and back, and becomes so cold and rigid he can be rolled like a ball. He may stay like this for as long as six months.

Most cold-blooded vertebrates, such as snakes and tortoises, hibernate, creeping alone into sheltered corners or crevices in the ground. Invertebrate snails gather together in heaps to keep each other warm.

In hot regions, many water creatures aestivate – 'summer sleep'. This seems to be triggered off by shortage of water. During long dry spells, crocodiles and alligators will bury themselves in the mud until rain fills the watercourse again. Some swamp fish do the same, and in Australia frogs have been known to aestivate in an underground cavern for as long as eighteen months.

Why do they say 'Mad as a March hare'?

The hare's rutting season is during February and March – April in the north of Scotland – and this makes them particularly wild and shy. They dash about, sometimes in circles, and occasionally two bucks will sit on their hindpaws and box each other with their forepaws.

Erasmus, the Renaissance philosopher, said 'Mad as a marsh hare', and added: 'Hares are wilder in marshes, from the absence of hedges and cover.' Certainly at other times of the year hares often 'freeze' in ditches or tangled undergrowth and you may almost step on them before they dart from their sheltering place.

Why does the snake dance to the charmer's flute?

It is odd that the snake seems to dance when its master plays, for snakes have no external or middle ears. But they do have two inner ears, and with these pick up sound through ground vibrations. The sensation goes through the nerve-endings near the ribs to the spinal cord and so, through the tiny inner ears, to the brain.

As the charmer is playing his flute, he is tapping his foot – gently, quietly, in a non-aggressive way; the snake reacts to this, not to the music. But once the snake's head is out of the basket, the flute does play a part, for the snake follows its rhythmic movement with its eyes.

Why are some snakes poisonous and others not?

The most essential and time-consuming activity for a snake is the pursuit, capture and digestion of food. So it is the way in which various snakes capture their victims that makes the difference.

Poisonous snakes have salivary glands where the venom is made; and this clear straw-coloured liquid containing various poisons is injected into the victim through grooved or tubular teeth. It usually has a neurotoxic agent, which paralyses the prey, and sometimes a 'haemolytic' material that breaks up the blood corpuscles, too. By giving its prey such an injection, the snake ensures that the victim will die almost immediately, or at least in a place not very far away. The snake *Bothrops insularis* on the Queimada Island off Brazil has a very fast-killing poison; this is because its food is mainly birds. If the venom took too long to act the bird would be able to fly away before it fell. But a relatively slow-moving land-born victim, once bitten, can be tracked down by the snake wherever it tries to hide.

Other, non-poisonous snakes catch their food by different methods that do not rely so heavily on speed. The British grass snake has no poison, but it lives mainly on frogs and fish. Other small burrowing or tree-born snakes without poison fangs eat earthworms or slugs. The boas of tropical America and the pythons of Africa and the Indian continent take hold of their prey in their teeth then quickly wrap a series of body coils around it. These coils are then tightened until the prey is crushed and suffocates – then it is eaten whole. This group contains the largest snake of all – the Anaconda boa found in the Amazon basin. It can be as much as 7·5 metres (twenty-five feet) long.

The snake which has every kind of equipment for catching its prey is a species of viper, the rattlesnake. The rattler feeds on small mammals, which are highly alert and quick. To help locate them, the rattlesnake has a facial pit which can detect warm-blooded creatures nearby, and also a poison gland with a rotating and a tubular fang.

The only poisonous snake found in Britain is the adder, *Viper berus*. Its bite is not usually fatal to an adult human, though it can be serious in a small child or a dog. The best treatment is to keep the patient calm and take him to a doctor at once.

Why does a rattlesnake rattle?

Although the rattlesnake bite can kill a man, it rarely attacks humans or other large creatures and uses its rattle to warn these enemies off.

The rattle is formed by a series of rings at the end of the snake's tail that increases as the snake ages. All snakes shed their skins from time to time; when the rattler does this the horny end of its tail remains. With each new skin another ring is added to the rattle; and these clash together when the cornered snake puffs itself up and shakes its tail at an aggressor.

How good are a dog's senses?

The two senses which, compared with man's, are most highly developed in dogs are hearing and smell. Sound frequency (the number of pulses per second) is reckoned by a unit called the hertz. The highest note in the musical scale is 20,000 hertz (or Hz) and this is the limit of the human ear. But cats can hear at 25,000 Hz and dogs upward of 30,000 Hz. As a result, a dog will respond to a sound too high for even a child to hear, and we take advantage of this in special high-pitched dog whistles.

But smell is even more important to a dog. While man's world is a visual one, the dog's is primarily one of smells. The dog's nasal passages are arranged to allow a great volume of air to be drawn over the nose's sensitive lining. Rapid sniffing carries messages to the brain, where the scent is identified and the information stored away for future reference.

The most interesting smells, to a dog, are the practical ones: scents that identify other animals, like sweat, excrement, urine, and the smell of the sex organs. But he also likes the grassy smells, soil, and ripe, decaying odours.

How do fish breathe?

Most fish exchange oxygen for carbon dioxide by passing water through their gills. The gills lie behind and to the side of the mouth cavity and consist of fleshy filaments supported by the gill arches and filled with blood capillaries, which give them their bright red colour. Water taken in all the time through the mouth passes back between the gill bars and over the filaments, where the exchange of gases takes place. In most fish the gills are protected by a gill cover, but in sharks, rays and some older fossil fish species they have flaps instead.

Most fish also have a hydrostatic or ballast organ called a swim bladder. This lies in the body cavity just below the kidney and above the stomach and intestine. It follows the same developmental pattern as the lungs of land vertebrates and the two structures must have developed from the same historical organ in primitive sea creatures.

In several unrelated species of fish the bladder has grown into a specialized lung or breathing organ. Some are even obliged to breathe air and will die if they cannot. Others are *Dipneusti* or 'double breathers' and have both gills and these primitive lungs. The *Lepidosiren* of South America live in swamps and marshes and rise frequently to breathe. When the swamp dries up they curl up and sleep in a burrow, blocking its entrance with a plug of mud but leaving openings for air.

Why aren't fish at the bottom of the ocean crushed to death?

The general level of the ocean floor is about 4,000 metres (13,000 feet); but there are depths going down to 10,000 metres (33,000 feet). Pressure increases by one atmosphere for each ten metres (33 feet), so at 10,000 metres the pressure is about 1,000 atmospheres or approximately 940 kilogrammes per square centimetre (six tons per square inch).

It does seem strange that living creatures can withstand this, but in fact normal body fluids are practically incompressible and it is only fish with gas-filled swim bladders that would be affected. And most deep-sea fishes have lost this; animals can and do live in these abyssal regions. In or on the ooze of the deep-sea floor are sea-cucumbers, live sponges, anemones, bivalve molluscs, crabs, bristle-stars and sea-urchins. Above these are squid, deep-sea prawns and a great variety of fishes.

Why are some animals warm-blooded and others cold?

Many so-called cold-blooded creatures are not cold to the touch; but they have to control the temperature of their bodies by external factors, by moving between sun and shade – and when it is very cold they must hibernate.

By contrast, the warm-blooded creature is independent of its environment. It maintains its heat by burning fuel and can be ready for action in any weather. One might compare it to a car engine that is kept warm and ticking over. Warm-bloodedness did not arise until a late stage of evolution, and it only occurs in birds and mammals. It gives them a great advantage over their nearest rivals, the insects, which in cold weather literally cannot get off the ground.

How can a fly walk upside-down on the ceiling?

The small house fly, *Musca domestica*, is quite well-equipped for this. At the end of each of its six legs it has a pair of special little claws with between them a small pad of very fine hairs called *pulvillae*. These hairs are obliquely pointed and covered with a sticky substance secreted from a gland in the fly's body.

On a rough, craggy surface like the bark of a tree the fly will maintain its balance by clinging tightly with its claws, and the same goes for an unevenly surfaced ceiling. On a smoother surface such as glass the fly drags its feet along so that the hooked hairs of its *pulvillae* and the oily secretion provide sufficient tension to stop it falling off.

The fly is also something of an acrobat. It can twist its body and land on its feet the wrong way up!

What makes a glow-worm glow?

The glow-worm *Lampyris noctiluca* is not actually a worm but a beetle, belonging to the same family as the firefly. The female glow-worm has no wings and produces the greenish-white light on her tail to signify she is at home to flying males seeking a mate.

She does this with special enzymes called 'luciferases' which catalyse (or bring about) a chemical reaction to produce a light almost without heat – a process known as 'bioluminescence'.

There are other light-producing species apart from the glow-worm and firefly. They usually produce a green light, but one, the 'railroad worm', has a red headlamp as well.

Why are marsupials such as kangaroos found only in Australia?

Marsupials are primitive mammals that give birth to minute young. These then develop to normal 'baby' size in a *marsupium*, or pouch, around the nipples of the mother.

Australia has been isolated from other land masses longer than any other continent, and it seems likely that the split occurred after the marsupials had arrived but before the more developed placental mammals could drive them out. So they were able to evolve and fill every habitat in Australia, often paralleling placental types, so that cats, wolves, bears, mice, squirrels, anteaters, rabbits and badgers all exist in pouched form.

Australia also has another very primitive animal: the duck-billed platypus, a mammal that lays eggs.

Do elephants go to a burial-ground before they die?

Many people have tried to find the legendary 'graveyards' to which old elephants are said to go when near death, but no genuine one has been found. Some groups of buried elephant remains have been discovered but they are probably places where several elephants have been drowned in bogs or rivers or perhaps even poisoned by a polluted water supply.

Elephants do sometimes carry off the bones of their dead companions. They may gnaw them for the calcium and other minerals that they need for their bones, teeth and tusks.

Why do animals moult?

In many temperate climates the summer is fairly warm and the winter quite cold; so the animals need to change their fur or feathers in the spring and autumn to suit the conditions.

Hairs are produced by little pits in the skin called 'follicles'. Each follicle has a cycle: an active phase during which a hair is produced and then a resting phase when the hair is held firmly in the follicle but no longer grows. When an animal is about to moult, the follicle starts a new period of activity, a new hair starts to grow and at about the time it erupts through the skin surface the old hair is released and shed.

Moulting is timed by the seasons; and the important feature is not the change in temperature but the altering day length. Human hair follicles carry out a similar cycle and though in humans this is essentially a continuous process there does seem to be a remnant of seasonal control in it.

Are there really mermaids?

Yes, there are, but sadly the 'mermaids' of fact do not live up to the lovely sirens of fiction. The legend owes its origin to a special kind of aquatic mammal, aptly named *Sirenia*, or, more popularly, 'sea-cow'. One form, the steller, was quite 'human' in appearance; it became extinct in the eighteenth century, but the dugong still exists in the Red Sea, the Indian Ocean and off the coast of Australia.

The dugong has a torpedo-shaped body ending in a flattened fish-like tail or paddle, and a broad muzzle with very mobile expanding lips. The female is very maternal towards her single young, suckles it in a human position and cradles it in her flippers. She also makes noises very like our own, in light, lilting tones that carry far across the sea from the tropic shallows where she likes to bask.

How do electric eels function?

Blind but dangerous, electric eels constantly discharge brief electrical impulses lasting two to three millisecs, to find their way and to capture food in the water. They have no optic nerve so use these radar-like impulses to steer clear of obstacles and locate their prey. The current passes from the tail to the head, and the strongest shock is given when both ends of the eel are in contact with its victim.

The eel (which is not, accurately, an eel at all but a South American fish similar to the catfish or carp) has electric organs running down four-fifths of its body. They are rather like batteries and are divided into three sections. Each consists of a mass of thin, flat cells called electro-plates which are arranged in orderly parallel columns. Each cell faces in the same direction, with a nerve-fibre terminating on one face and not the other. There are about six thousand in each column, and in the whole fish there may be as many as three-quarters of a million of them. Each is capable of discharging about one-tenth of a volt, so *Electrophorus electricus* can produce discharges of 550 volts, enough to shock a man severely, or turn on a light bulb of several hundred watts.

The discharge is triggered off by an electro-chemical reaction. A difference of potential is built up between the two different faces of the cells, caused by sodium and potassium ions entering and exiting from the cells. These movements in and out produce different concentrations of ions in the cells and provide the immediate source of energy for the electrical discharge.

Do ants bite?

Yes, they not only bite but sometimes sting as well. They can inflict with their jaws a nasty little hole in the skin and then swing their abdomen round and squirt poison in. The most common venom is formic acid, a molecular compound of carbon, hydrogen and oxygen, smelling a bit like vinegar.

The sting consists of a pair of stylets which run inside a sheath and begin in the abdomen. The poison of the sting is made by a venom gland opening into the inner end of the sheath and released by muscular contraction. The ant bends its abdomen between its legs and can spray up to six droplets of about one milligramme (0·015 grain). The poison raises a blister that usually lasts for about ten days.

Are ants really as clever as they seem?

Yes, they are. There are ants that steal, ants that do acrobatics, ants that carve up wood and ants that pasture aphids or greenfly like we do cattle. But one of the most fascinating is the 'atta' or parasol ant, for, in their secret subterranean labyrinths they farm – an activity that no other creature performs, apart from the termite (a close relative of the ant) and man.

The gardening process begins just after the winged princess and the male fly off to mate. She carries in a special pouch behind her jaws a dowry consisting of a little hoard of fungus spores. After mating in mid-air, the queen drops to the ground and tears off her wings; then runs round looking for a new, moist home in the ground. She ejects her fungus spores and prunes the first crop as it grows, licking it to keep it moist and at the same time laying her first eggs. As the eggs hatch they feed on her cultivated fungus, and once the workers are adult they take over care of the garden.

Marching out of the nest, they file up plants and trees, cutting leaves and petals with their mandibles. These pieces, carried home like parasols, are used as fertilizer. The ants chew them finely and urinate on them to speed the compost process. In time, the crops are laid out in galleries, and the fungus is repeatedly pruned to prevent it reaching fruiting or toadstool stage. It is encouraged to form tiny knots about the size of a pinhead; these are weeded and eaten by the ants.

And the amounts are carefully rationed out, to produce the different castes of ant. Those allowed very little never grow to be more than small workers that tend the garden in the nest. A medium-rich diet nourishes the questing ants that strip and carry leaves, while even more food is allowed to the soldier ants that defend the nest. But the best food of all goes to the idle males and to the winged princess that will emerge and gather spores, then fly off to mate and become a queen in her own right.

Why do locusts swarm?

It is probably because of over-population. Certainly, Sir Boris Uvarov discovered about fifty years ago that what were once thought to be solitary grasshoppers and swarming locusts are in fact various species of the same creature, in single and migratory phases. In the past, they have been very destructive and have travelled great distances. In 1869, members of a swarm originating in West Africa reached England in considerable numbers. But recently, cultivation of their breeding grounds has tended to keep the numbers down.

What is the shiny substance left behind by a snail?

It is mucus, secreted by the 'paedal glands' on the foot at the front end of the snail. Its purpose is to lubricate the foot and also to help adhesion. Snails prefer damp conditions and are most active at night and during and after rainfall. On dry, hot days, they tend to hide away, or aestivate.

What makes a jumping bean jump?

It is not actually a bean but the fruit of a shrub called 'yerba de flecha', the poisoned-arrow plant, which grows in arid parts of Mexico. And it jumps because inside the bean there is a caterpillar jerking about.

It is the larva of the moth *Carpocapsa saltitans*, which lays its egg when the flowers appear in early summer. The grub hatches inside the 'bean' which provides it with food for several months. Too much heat would destroy it, so under strong sunlight the grub flexes its body and flips the bean forward, perhaps even for several centimetres at one hop.

Before pupating, the caterpillar cuts a circular door in the bean's shell, and in the spring the pupa emerges from this, ready to become a moth.

But, alas for the moths of the jumping beans in our toyshops, there are no poisoned-arrow plants ready to receive their eggs.

How do chameleons change their colour?

Chameleons do change colour, but only within a fairly limited colour range, and they respond more to emotion or light-intensity than to their background.

Most chameleons (there are about eighty different species) can vary their skin colour from yellow to green to brown and black. They are at their palest (usually yellow) when they are asleep or totally in the dark, while green is their palest waking colour. They go dark – i.e. brownish-black, when exposed to bright light. When chameleons wake up they look for a patch of sunlight, and the side of their body exposed to the sun turns dark while that in the shade stays green. When they return to the shade they become green all over. These colour changes are fairly slow and take up to a quarter of an hour. By contrast, when chameleons are emotionally disturbed they display a dark-spotted pattern within seconds. This usually happens when they are confronted by a predator or when another chameleon invades their territory.

The colour cells lie under the chameleon's transparent skin in three layers. The outer layer comprises yellow pigment cells called 'lipophores', and the second layer consists of iridescent plate-like crystals ('guanophotes') which are able to reflect white and blue light. Beneath are cells which contain the black pigment 'melanin'. These have tentacles up through the two layers above, through which the melanin granules can rise.

The colour changes are stimulated by nerves in the chameleon's skin. When it lies totally relaxed, the black melanin granules remain at the base of the cells. White light is reflected from the guanophotes and the chameleon appears yellow because of the top layer of yellow pigment. When the melanin cells are stimulated and the granules rise to the base of the iridescent crystal guanophotes, they absorb all colours except blue – on the same principle that dust particles make the sky look blue. This blue, mixed with the yellow lipophores, gives the chameleon a green coloration. Finally, if the chameleon is so stimulated that the black pigment travels all the way up the tentacles, the other two layers are totally obscured.

Many other animals can change their colour. Some fish, like the turbot and the plaice, can do the job so effectively that if you put one on a draughts board it will make its body a passable imitation of the chequered pattern. And a squid, when disturbed, blushes all over with colour as spots flash on and off very rapidly. But the mechanism is rather different from that of the chameleon: the squid's pigment cells are expanded by muscle contraction.

Does a bee die after using its sting?

Yes it does, if its victim was a person, for its sting is really adapted for use against other insects. It can withdraw its sting from their soft intersegmental membranes but in firm human flesh the barbed shaft becomes embedded and tears part of the bee's abdomen away.

The sting mechanism is similar in structure to an egg-laying organ called an 'ovipositor' which is used by other insects to pierce holes in plant tissues, other insects, even hard wood, in which the insect deposits its eggs. In the bee this organ has been adjusted to inject poison instead. It is contained within a chamber at the end of the abdomen, from which protrudes the familiar tapering, sharp-pointed shaft.

When the bee stings it usually takes hold of its victim with its claws, then bends its abdomen abruptly downwards so that the tip of the out-thrust shaft is inserted into the victim's flesh. Poison is channelled through the shaft by muscular contraction.

Usually the sting results in a painful inflammation, but some people claim that the poison is helpful against diseases like rheumatism and arthritis.

What is smell?

Smell, or 'olfaction', is the detection and identification by sensory organs of airborne chemicals: chemo-reception. However, invertebrates and lower vertebrates (fish, reptiles and amphibians) rarely have a nose. These lower animals detect chemicals in their surroundings by means of receptors in various parts of the body; a snake, for example, uses its tongue.

In man and the higher vertebrates, olfaction depends mainly on chemically sensitive nerves in the lining of the nasal cavity. Mammals which rely heavily on smell for locating food or for warning against predators have very finely developed noses. The bones supporting the nasal cavity are turbinal, or shaped like a whirling top, to give a large area for sniffing the air.

What is rabies?

Rabies, or 'hydrophobia', is a virus disease that occurs in many animals and is transmitted by bites. The incubation period is roughly two months – but this varies considerably and can be as long as eight months. The disease has been stamped out in Britain by the strict enforcement of quarantine laws, but in Europe it is spreading and may soon reach the Channel coast.

When the patient feels the first symptoms, he is irritable and excited, with painful muscle spasms. These are brought on by the act of swallowing, and this has led to the belief that the victim fears water, whereas in fact he is plagued by thirst. Patients may become maniacal and even try to bite their helpers; eventually they become paralysed and die of heart failure in about five days. Cases of rabies are very rarely cured once the symptoms have begun to show, but it is possible to have a course of injections to prevent the virus taking hold. These are given deep in the tissues of the belly and are made from material taken from the spinal cords of infected rabbits. But even these injections are most painful and unpleasant: rabies is not a disease to be taken lightly at all.

Why do we cry when peeling onions?

Onions contain several volatile sulphur compounds: methyl disulphide, methyl trisulphide, methyl-n-propyl trisulphide, n-propyl disulphide and n-propyl trisulphide, to be precise! When these harsh chemical vapours are released into the air, they irritate our eyes, which water to wash the chemicals from the surface of the eyeball.

So it follows that, if you peel onions under water, the vapours don't get into the air, and you won't cry.

What causes white spots and ridges on fingernails?

The white spots usually occur when the matrix area at the base is damaged while the nail is forming or 'keratinizing' underneath. Horny ridges happen when something stimulates the normally sterile nail bed into action, perhaps pressure or a blow. It assumes keratinizing activities for a while, creating a thickened or deformed nail.

What happens when a fingernail goes black?

The blackness is a layer of blood under the nail that has been released by squashing or banging the finger. It cannot escape and stays beneath the surface rather like a bruise. The best treatment for a severe case is to release the pressure: ask a doctor to drill or burn a small hole through the nail. Otherwise the nail will probably be forced off, leaving a sore, exposed nail bed until the new nail has grown up.

Why do I hiccup?

Perhaps because you have drunk too much fizzy lemonade! Certainly, in an experiment in the *Don't Ask Me* studio, Dr Miriam Stoppard found she had an excellent response rate to this 'treatment'. Curing the hiccups proved rather more difficult, however, though in nearly all cases they will eventually simply go away. They are caused by irritation of the nerves supplying the diaphragm; the diaphragm muscles suddenly contract to create an abrupt indrawing of air that ends in a click made by the vocal cords as they snap shut.

Some of the cures people recommend: a sudden fright, drinking water from the wrong side of a glass, drinking lots of water or small quantities of peppermint water, spirits or alkalis, and – perhaps the most effective – breathing in carbon dioxide. You can do this by holding a paper bag to your mouth and breathing in and out. Don't do it with a plastic bag: you could suffocate.

Why have people got different-coloured skins?

Skin colour is caused partly by blood vessels near the surface – the colour showing through – but mainly by the pigment 'melanin' manufactured in the skin. It seems to be a protective substance, which would explain why the people from hot countries tend to have the darker skins, and also why light-skinned people tan; but there are remarkable variations, even among members of the same race or family.

Melanin is manufactured by special cells called 'melanocytes' which lie below or between the deepest cells of the skin, the 'dermis'. They have long, thin, streamer-like tendrils that worm their way between the epidermal cells. The melanin is produced in the 'cytoplasm' at the base of the centre of the melanocyte and sent out to its tendrils or 'dendrites', which are tree-like in shape. Then skin cells in contact with these melanin-laden areas absorb the pigment into themselves, and when they are exposed to ultra-violet light (sunlight) the melanin granules move to form a protective sheath over the nucleus of the skin cell.

So it does seem that both the tanning of skin in strong sunlight and the various natural colourings are all due to the activity of melanin in the skin. And, curiously, everyone, fair or dark, has roughly the same number of melanocytes in each area. They simply vary in type and activity to produce the differences of colour.

Why are there so many accents?

Accents or dialects are variations of a language that differ from one another in their sound systems, word and sentence patterns or vocabulary. The two main types are geographic dialects, spoken by people from the same area, and social accents, used by people of the same class, educational level or job. But people may in fact adopt several different dialects or accents, following the pattern accepted at home, school or employment.

All languages change; and because they are extremely complex sign systems they change in different ways as they are affected by outside influences and ideas. The Old English or Anglo-Saxon of the eighth-century poem *Beowulf* seems like a foreign language to us because since that time Latin, French and other foreign words and language structures have been introduced. At the same time the original grammar or language skeleton has been simplified by everyday use. But the process was different in the various areas where the same basic language was in use. So in the north of Britain more Norse words and grammatical forms have survived; the English of Wales and Cornwall has a strong Celtic influence, while in America the original Elizabethan English of the early settlers has developed its own pronunciation, colourful variants and spelling system.

Writing, and recently radio and television, have worked against this trend, so that so-called Standard English is now used or at least understood almost nationwide. It is essentially the language of the old southern, richer and educated classes, who wrote and travelled widely and so made their influence felt. But dialect and accent variations help reflect a nation's history as well as being attractive and colourful in themselves; and it is good to keep them, for they help us to communicate in a vivid and interesting way.

Why does alcohol make you drunk?

Because it is a drug that affects the central nervous system. It belongs to the same class as the barbiturates, minor tranquillizers and general anaesthetics and is, in fact, a depressant. Its effect on the brain has two phases: at quite low concentrations it can serve as an excitant or stimulant of some functions because normal inhibiting factors that restrict behaviour are suppressed. But as the concentration increases, depressive factors take over. The drinker's mind becomes dull and stupefied; he may even fall into a coma. Death can result if the breathing centres of the brain or the heart become anaesthetized – but in a healthy man this happens only if he drinks and absorbs as much as a litre (nearly two pints) of alcohol 50° proof.

What is sleeping sickness?

It is a tropical disease, still fairly common in Africa, caused by parasites called 'Trypanosomes' and transmitted from one victim to another by the tsetse fly. Game animals, horses and cattle suffer from it as well

33

as man. It is called sleeping sickness because in the final stages the victim becomes very apathetic and tends to doze all day.

There is also 'sleepy sickness', which is a disease of the brain called *Encephalitis lethargica*, in which the patient suffers from double vision.

What are freckles?

A freckle or 'ephelis' is a small, brownish, well-defined stain or spot on the skin that occurs most frequently in people who are fair. It happens because the melanocyte pigment cells of their skin respond only slightly, and unevenly, to sunlight. So the fair skin hardly tans at all, and any melanin pigment that is manufactured is laid down irregularly to create a multitude of freckles instead. They usually appear after the age of five and tend to fade in the winter. Apart from avoiding sunlight, there is no known way of preventing them, but they are quite harmless and lots of people think they are attractive.

What are allergies?

Allergies are caused by the body's reaction to substances outside itself. Most people react slightly to materials like pollen and dust, but the allergic person's body responds far more fiercely.

Allergy-causing substances are usually proteins. They may be contained in certain foods, in washing powders or in drugs. Some people are allergic to nylon or woollen clothes. Others can suffer severely from a bee or mosquito bite.

When the body first encounters a substance or 'antigen' it does not like, it produces antibodies in case it meets that antigen again. Normally, this is just a useful protective device, but in the allergic person the response goes too far. Cells affected by the interaction of antigen and antibody give off certain chemicals – histamine is the most common of these – and they are responsible for the lumps, rash, itchy eyes or streaming nose that are the obvious symptoms of an allergic attack. Drugs designed to counter the effects of histamine – antihistamines – sometimes relieve the symptoms; but they cannot cure their cause. For this the body needs a course of injections by which it is desensitized. But this is a long process and hardly worthwhile if the antigen can be avoided or if the allergy is only troublesome for short periods of the year.

Why do they say you won't catch mumps or measles twice?

Actually you can, with mumps at least, if you have it the first time only in the glands on one side of your neck. But normally this rule does apply because the body acquires an immunity to infections to which it has been once exposed.

When the alien virus makes its attack the body produces antibodies which remain for life in the blood supply. If the same virus tries to take hold again the antibodies go into action, destroying the virus before it makes the person ill. This defence mechanism can even be passed on from a mother to her baby, but only lasts in the child a short while.

Some viruses, particularly those that cause influenza or the common cold, have the power to mutate or change a little as time goes by. When the new model makes its invasion the body's antibodies do not recognize it – and we are sneezing again, with yet another cold!

Why do people go bald?

Not many women do, but hereditary baldness is fairly common in men. It is probably caused by the male hormones in the bloodstream,

and some recent research has indicated that the amount of cholesterol in the blood influences baldness as well. There is no real cure, although so-called hair restorers may help by getting the remaining hair in good condition.

Some acute fevers may also cause the hair to fall out; this can happen to women as well as men. But it usually grows back when the patient is well again. And you could lose your hair as a result of shock – then it might grow back lighter in colour, or even white.

Why do we blink?

Blinking is involuntary; we do not think about it, but actually blink all the time. The rate varies: more often when the light is bright, and less when soft-toned objects are in sight. The movement washes down an antiseptic and cleaning fluid produced by the lachrymal gland under the upper eyelid; this helps our eyes in all sorts of ways. They must reflect light, and can only do this when there is moisture on the surface. The cornea, the small translucent coloured front of the eye, has no blood vessels, and without the bathing in antiseptic fluid, ulcers would develop there. It also washes off particles of dust and comforts the eye in strong winds or when the air is very dry. And in cold weather frequent blinking helps to keep the eye warm. Lastly, the muscular action of blinking keeps the muscles of the eye in trim, while the momentary closing gives the tiny muscles of the pupil a chance to relax their tension.

Why do we have an appendix?

It is odd, because the appendix is useless to man and can become a great nuisance. It is a hollow, narrow, muscular tube, seven to nine centimetres (three to four inches) long and less than one centimetre (about half an inch) wide, which emerges from the 'caecum' – the large intestine. The narrow entrance to the appendix from the caecum easily becomes blocked, and if infection or appendicitis sets in, the appendix has to be removed by surgery.

Some mammals such as the higher apes, wombats, civets and rodents find their appendix quite useful. Their diet contains a good deal more cellulose than man eats nowadays, and this cellulose is trapped in the appendix and digested there over a long period. Probably man once used his appendix like this as well, but it is now gradually disappearing – becoming a vestigial organ – now that he does not need it any more.

What causes 'butterflies' in the stomach?

When we are startled or frightened, preparing for a challenge like running a mile in 3·50 or jumping across a gap, or just asking out someone we fancy, adrenalin enters our blood system.

Adrenalin is a hormone secreted by the 'medulla' – the centre part of the glands above the kidney – and it prepares the body for the sort of emergency or challenge described above. It stimulates the pulse rate and increases the blood supply to the muscles so that they can cope. But less blood flows to the digestive organs (causing those butterflies) and to the skin, so we may also turn pale with fright. At the same time the adrenalin transforms glycogen in the liver into glucose to provide quick energy.

What is colour-blindness?

Only man and the other primates, some insects, fish, amphibia, some reptiles and some birds can see in colour. Human beings have three types of cones in the retina – the light-sensitive layer of tissue that lines the back and sides of the eyeball. One kind of cone absorbs light best in wavelengths of blue-violet and another in wavelengths of green. The third is most sensitive to yellow wavelengths but also reacts to red. And it is when these cones are faulty that colour-blindness occurs.

Three colours are involved – red, green and blue – and people may be unable to see one, two or all three of them. Blindness to red is called 'protanopia'; blindness to green 'deuteranopia' and blindness to blue 'tritanopia'. People who are red-blind are unable to distinguish between red and green, while blue-blind people cannot distinguish between blue and yellow. Green-blind people simply do not see the green part of the spectrum.

Colour-blindness may be caused by disease or injury of the optic nervous system, but blindness to red and green are more commonly inherited and affect about twenty times as many boys as girls. The characteristic is sex-linked and recessive; it usually skips a generation because it is carried by the female line. This means that the daughter of a colour-blind man and a normal woman will pass the characteristic on – her sons will be colour-blind and her own daughters will carry the trait. But the sons of a normal woman and a colour-blind man will not be affected, nor will they pass on the characteristic. And it is only if a girl's father is colour-blind and her mother a carrier as well that she herself will suffer from it.

Why do we dream?

Probably in order to work out problems and worries that we never face fully in our waking life. People seem to need to dream, and, if their dreaming sleep is disturbed, will spend more time dreaming the next night. But in the morning we often forget that we have been dreaming at all.

In 1953, a new era of dream research began when it was noticed that rapid eye movements behind the closed lids of a sleeping person are accompanied by faster breathing and additional electrical activity in the brain, all of which signal the fact that the sleeper is dreaming. Usually the dream lasts only for five to ten minutes. It is followed by a quiet period and then by another active one – three or four altogether in the night.

When people are woken during rapid eye movement they tend to report vivid dreams while those disturbed when sleeping quietly have no dream to recount. And if a sleeper is woken every time he begins to show signs of dreaming he will go through these dream movements more frequently the next night.

What is cramp?

Cramp is a painful involuntary spasmodic contraction of the muscles. It is usually felt in the limbs but some internal organs can be affected.

Swimmer's cramp is caused by over-exertion. The pain is literally crippling, and the swimmer may drown unless he is rescued quickly. But people also wake in the night suffering from severe cramp in the calf of the leg. In old people, this is probably caused by poor circulation, and cramp in general does seem to be linked to some deficiency in the blood supply in relation to a muscle's activity. Perhaps the sleeper has overstretched the leg, or taken too much exercise the previous day. Hardening of the arteries has the same effect. Cramp may develop after walking only a short distance. A brief stop relieves it, but it will return after another short walk.

Heat cramps are due to loss of salt after sweating heavily. Over-exertion in a hot environment is usually responsible for this. And there really is a writer's cramp. Musicians, typists, seamstresses, painters and telephone operators can all suffer in a similar way. They find it increasingly difficult to use the instrument, keyboard, needle – whatever is the tool of their particular trade – but the same muscles work quite naturally to do something else.

Why do feet smell?

Because of perspiration, or sweat. Sweat is secreted by tiny sweat glands scattered all over the surface of our bodies and through them we lose over a pint of liquid a day. We sweat more when our own temperature or the temperature outside rises, in order to cool our bodies. Since the sweat glands are most numerous on the palms of the hands, the groin, the armpits and the soles of the feet, it is no wonder your feet smell if you don't wash them or your socks.

Sweat is mostly water but it contains about 2 per cent solids: salts, small amounts of fat and urea – excreted by the kidneys as waste. It is mostly this urea which causes the 'bromidrosis', or bad-smelling sweat, when bacterial decomposition sets in after the sweat is exposed to the air.

The odour of sweat is altered to quite a recognizable degree in various diseases. Doctors use this in diagnosis: the sour smell of rheumatism, the smell of fear in neurotics, the unpleasant sweetish odour of dyspepsia. And it is believed that animals can scent the sweat of fear. Sweat can even be coloured – blue from taking indigo, and red in certain blood conditions (which may explain the saying 'sweating blood').

What are bruises?

They are marks that show bleeding beneath the skin. Bruises are usually the result of a blow with a blunt instrument or the human fist, but they may happen after a fall, especially in older people, whose blood-vessels are more easily broken.

The 'black and blue' mark is in fact a slight haemorrhage. It usually shows up in the area of actual injury but may appear further down the body. So a blow on the shoulder may lead to a black patch in the region of the loins, or a knock on the buttocks cause a blue mark on the calf of the leg. The colouring eventually fades away, changing from black to bluish and then to brown and yellow.

Most bruises can be ignored completely. They simply go away; and treating them with expensive cuts of steak does not particularly help – a cold-water compress is just as comforting. But if you fear that the bruise is part of a more serious injury, such as a broken bone, you should ask for medical help.

What are moles on the skin?

A mole is a pigmented, flat or fleshy skin lesion made up of a collection of melanocytes – the cells that synthesize the skin pigment melanin. Thicker lesions also have nerve elements and connective tissue.

Surface moles vary in colour from light to dark brown; but when the melanin cells group together in the dermis (the deeper layer of skin underneath the epidermis on the surface) the lesion has a bluish tint.

Moles may be present when you are born, but they more often appear and evolve in childhood or later in life. A new mole is usually flat and of the junctional type – because it is located between the dermis and the epidermis. It sometimes remains there, in which case it just might become malignant. But it is more likely to evolve into a slightly raised bump on the surface of the skin, which is harmless.

What are birthmarks?

Birthmarks, or 'naevi' as they are called, are made up of a tangled mass of blood vessels, created in the baby's early development. One of the most common forms is the 'port wine stain' or 'mother's mark'. Birthmarks are of course most noticeable when they occur on the face, but they can be anywhere. If they are ugly or seem likely to grow, they can be removed by surgery or electrolysis; but they are usually harmless.

What are warts?

Warts or 'verrucae' are small growths on the surface of the skin which are caused by a virus. The most common type is a round raised lesion with a dry rough surface, but flat or threadlike ones are also seen. They sometimes occur singly, but often, particularly in small children, a crop of them may appear – only to disappear with equal suddenness. This has led to the belief that warts can be charmed away, but really the verrucae disappear because the body develops antibodies to defeat the relevant virus. In any case, they are usually painless unless they grow on pressure areas, like plantar warts on the sole of the foot.

Why do people smoke?

Tobacco smoking was first practised by North and South American Indians. They used it in ceremonials – 'the pipe of peace' – and also believed it had medicinal properties. It was introduced into Europe by Christopher Columbus, Sir Walter Raleigh and other explorers.

Over the years all sorts of social, religious and medical arguments have been used against the habit. It is clearly associated with lung cancer, coronary thrombosis, hardening of the arteries, chronic bronchitis, emphysema and, for pipe smokers, cancer of the lip; but the habit is world wide.

Most young people who start smoking begin in middle or late adolescence, with those in manual jobs tending to smoke earlier in life. Intelligence seems to make no difference to the statistics as to who does and does not smoke. The first cigarette is probably taken out of curiosity, a desire to conform, to seem grown up; and advertising and the example of parents are influential also.

Once smoking starts, people become addicted to the nicotine and related alkaloids in tobacco, for nicotine is a stimulant drug. They find it comforting, too, to have something in the mouth, and find smoking reduces tension, helps them to think and to behave naturally in a potentially frightening situation. But smoking is very damaging. Governments all over the world are trying to discourage young people from taking up the habit, and to limit consumption by imposing high taxes, extending 'no smoking' areas, and by using propaganda.

Why do we get wrinkles in old age?

It is because the elastic component of the skin, called 'collagen', deteriorates – rather like knicker elastic that has been washed too often. Collagen lies in bundles of fibres in the deeper layer of the skin, and it can be damaged by ultra-violet penetration (sunlight). So there was a scientific basis for the Victorian parasol. Usually men have 15 per cent more collagen fibres than women, and black people tend to have more than white.

Most cosmetic products do nothing more than trap moisture in the skin for a short time, but damaged collagen fibres can be replaced artificially by injections of silicon in a gel form.

Why do some foods make the mouth water?

The salivary glands are constantly secreting. There are six of them: two in the throat, two in the cheeks and two underneath the tongue. In addition, a lot of little glands are dispersed on the underside of the lips and cheeks.

Saliva is alkaline and it also contains antibodies which help to keep down mouth bacteria; but its main function is to start off the process of digestion.

When we put food into the mouth, three factors work in turn to make the saliva flow. The taste buds on the tongue send nerve messages to the brain which in turn activate the salivary glands. They respond particularly to acid, salt and sweetness. In addition, texture, like the crispness of nuts or celery, increases the flow of saliva, and so does the very action of chewing. Even chewing on a rubber band will cause the mouth to water.

But what about the smell of a really tasty meal? It only makes us aware of the saliva already in our mouths. Normally we do not notice it – except when the supply is cut off in conditions of tension or fear.

Why do we panic?

Panic is an extreme emotion: an exaggeration of our normal reaction to danger, which we have inherited from our animal ancestors and which is geared to survival.

When we observe, or imagine, something dangerous, the brain sends messages all over the body; resulting in increased heartbeat, deeper breathing, excess sweating, tenser muscles and dilated pupils in the eyes. We also get an increased flow of adrenalin, making us alert and ready for violent action throughout our system. All these panic symptoms prepare the body to run away or to stand and fight.

Do carrots help you to see in the dark?

There is a little truth in this, because carrots contain a lot of vitamin A and if you are short of this you may suffer from 'hemeralopia', difficulty in adjusting to twilight after being in a bright light. This happens because the cells of the eye particularly concerned with detecting low light intensities, known as rods, contain a pigment called rhodopsin, or 'visual purple', that is derived from vitamin A.

But most cases of poor sight have nothing at all to do with a deficiency of vitamin A. The idea gained currency because hemeralopia was discovered just about the time of the Battle of Britain; and at the same time the British were introducing radar, which did seem to make pilots able to see in the dark. To keep radar a secret, the propaganda service spread stories about RAF pilots eating plates of carrots – and I daresay there was a glut of carrots about just then as well.

The whole story is rather interesting, because it illustrates just how easy it is to create a new old wives' tale!

Why does the weather affect our moods?

On those muggy days before a storm it's not necessarily the moisture in the air that makes us feel irritable; the air is also full of positive ions of atmospheric electricity. And positive ions are known to make us feel literally under the weather.

But climate can have a depressing effect, too. The basic work on the effects of ions on human health has been done in Jerusalem, where a hot dry wind called the 'chamssin' blows in from the Arabian desert. It causes a high positive ion concentration in the atmosphere – and 75 per cent of the population experience irritability, headaches, listlessness and depression.

Dr Felix Sulman of the Hebrew University in Jerusalem has discovered that the release of a hormone called 'serotonin' is stimulated by an excess of positive ions in the air we breathe. And this hormone acts on the brain to cause what he calls the 'irritation syndrome' by influencing sleep and the nervous system generally. In contrast, negative ions in the atmosphere reduce the level of serotonin and produce feelings of calmness and well-being.

That is why we feel so good after the storm passes; for a short time there is an excess of negative ions. This is nearly always the case on the coast and in mountain regions, which is why we find these places so pleasant and bracing.

How do flowers know when to bloom?

Some flowers do not seem to mind the season, so long as they have warmth, light, water and nutrients: when the plant has reached a certain stage of maturity, out come the flowers. In others, flowering can only occur after the plant has been exposed to low temperatures – what the botanists call 'vernalization'. This applies to spring-flowering plants like wallflowers, violets and primroses, where the buds are actually induced by the cold winter weather and the flowers appear as soon as the days warm up in the spring.

But in many plants, flowering is controlled by a process called photoperiodism. 'Photo' means light, and when this phenomenon was first investigated in 1920 it was thought that the length of daylight was the deciding factor. But we now know it is the longer or shorter nights that are important.

Typical summer plants like petunias, antirrhinums, fuchsias and carnations will only flower when the night is short. Others, such as chrysanthemums, poinsettia and the Christmas cactus need long nights and short days; and they will not flower, even in the autumn or winter, if their long night is interrupted by artificial light.

This dependence on day length has been exploited commercially, particularly with chrysanthemums, which only flower when the day length is less than fourteen hours. Black polythene covers are drawn over the beds during the summer months; or in the winter, when the 'mums' would normally bloom, flowering is delayed by putting lights on in the night.

It looks as though plants like chrysanthemums have a biological clock which can measure time. The leaves contain a light-sensitive pigment called phytochrome which, when it receives the correct light/dark sequence, releases a chemical messenger that is transported up the stem. This stimulus is a plant hormone, but although it has been given the hypothetical name 'florigen' no one has managed to isolate it yet.

Why are flowers scented and brightly coloured?

Plants need to attract the agents of pollination. Unless the flower is pollinated it will not form a seed box and cannot reproduce. So it has developed ways to attract the creatures that carry pollen from the male organ or stamen of one flower, to the female pistil of another.

Plants have evolved these attracting devices in different ways. Some bloom only in the morning or for an hour or so at midday. The flowers of the antirrhinum or snapdragon and those of the pea family will only open fully if the appropriate insect treads in just the right place. Then its body must brush against the stamens and carry pollen on to the pistil of the next flower. The night-scented stock, *Matthiola bicornia*, looks straggly and insignificant in bright sunlight, but when it is dark the small purple flowers open and scent the air all around.

For the plant is fertilized by moths, not by insects that fly during the day; so it saves its resources until the appropriate time.

What is pollination?

Plants must be pollinated if they are to reproduce. Pollen is produced by the stamens, the male part of the flower, and is transferred in pollination to the female ovules, where the seed forms. In conifers (fir trees and pines) or cycads (palms), where the ovule is exposed, the pollen is simply caught in a drop of fluid secreted by the ovule. But in flowering plants the ovule is contained inside a hollow organ called the pistil, and the pollen is deposited on the pistil's receptive surface, the stigma.

Because plants cannot move about to fertilize themselves, all kinds of outside agents are used to carry the pollen about. Insects are the most common – think of the bee's furry breeches laden with pollen – but with different plants the wind, birds, mammals and water each play a part.

Do insectivorous plants really devour their victims?

There are about 180 species of insect-eating plants. They tend to grow in damp heaths, bogs and marshes where normal plant nutrients are in poor supply. In general, their leaves are adapted to capture insects and other tiny creatures attracted by the plant's nectar or colour.

The pitcher plant or monkey cup lures its prey with a sweet secretion on the stem and rim of the leaf 'pitcher', and also inside the cup itself. As the insect leans over the corrugated rim to sip this delicious nectar it loses its footing on the crumbly wax surface that lines the upper half of the trap and falls into the liquid below. Its struggles then stimulate the plant to secrete an acid and a protein-dissolving enzyme, and it digests and absorbs the animal nutrients. The size of the pitcher varies a great deal – from a thimble to a quart pot – but luckily none of them would ensnare a man!

The leaves of the sundew form a rosette at the base of the plant and are covered with filaments or tentacles (about two hundred on each leaf) which produce a sticky substance. A fly landing on this surface

sticks, and the hairs bend to pass it to the centre of the leaf, secreting more liquid all the time. It may take several days for the insect to be digested; then the leaf re-opens and the trap is re-set. In Portugal, cottagers hang branches of a plant allied to the sundew, *Drosophyllum lusitanicum*, in their houses. The long narrow leaves do not move but are covered by a sticky substance, and work like flypapers to attract and trap the flies.

In the Venus fly-trap each leaf consists of two lobes, hinged together like a man-trap with spiny teeth. Pressure-sensitive hairs in the centre of each lobe trigger off the closing mechanism when the victim alights. The trap closes very quickly – under normal conditions it takes about half a second, but speeds as fast as one-tenth of a second have been recorded.

What are algae?

They are primitive, plant-like water organisms that range in size from single-cell forms to large seaweeds, and there are as many as twenty-five thousand of them. They are capable of photosynthesis but they do not have true leaves, stems, roots or vascular systems. All the same, they are extremely valuable as primary producers of food; for they start the chain that in the end feeds all water creatures.

What are lichens?

They are really very odd: a unique mixture of algae and fungi. This gives them a plant structure that can flourish in climates where the two separate elements could not live. The cells of the algae provide food by photosynthesis while the fungi threads absorb water vapour from the air and minute quantities of minerals from the rocks they cling to. But many lichens cannot survive in dirty, polluted air.

Some lichens are edible. 'Reindeer moss' provides food for wild reindeer in the Arctic tundra and is also harvested for cattle; and it is even said that the manna which saved the children of Israel in the Bible was a mountain lichen. Lichen can be used to make dyes, and this is still done on the island of Harris in the Hebrides.

What is moss?

Moss and liverworts are among the simplest plants and are in many ways the land equivalent of water algae. They flourish all over the world, wherever there is enough moisture.

Liverworts often form flat growths like bright green pancakes on the damp sides of banks, in ditches or on neglected walls. They are very simple in structure and reproduce like fungi by the means of windblown spores.

Mosses are more complicated, as they have stems, leaves and a root-like structure; but they also reproduce by spores. There are roughly fifteen thousand species in more than six hundred genera, and they range in size from microscopic forms to plants more than a metre long. One Australian moss even grows forty-five centimetres (eighteen inches) high. The most common moss in Britain is the bog- or peat-moss called sphagnum. It likes a great deal of water and covers enormous areas in moist temperate and cool regions, where it eventually forms a poor, brownish-coloured peat.

What is peat?

Peat is organic fuel that varies from a light spongy material mainly composed of sphagnum moss in the upper layers of bogs, to a dense, dark-brown, wetter substance at the bog bottom. It forms where the

49

drainage is bad, as dead plants accumulate and partly decompose. There are vast deposits in Europe, North America and Asia.

Peat is the first step in the formation of coal. The humid climate of the Carboniferous period three hundred million years ago favoured the growth of huge tropical seed ferns and giant non-flowering trees, and created the swamp areas that comprise the peat and coal beds of today. As the plants died and fell into the boggy waters, which excluded oxygen and killed bacteria, they did not entirely rot away. Slowly, the vegetation was changed into peat, some brown and spongy, some black and compact, depending on the degree of compression and decomposition. The sea advanced and withdrew, leaving new layers of sediment on top. In some cases, glaciers deposited further layers of soil and compressed the peat with their weight. If there was enough pressure, the peat dried and hardened to become low-grade coal or lignite; more pressure and time created bituminous coal and finally anthracite.

What is a papaw?

It is a deciduous tree of the custard-apple family and a native of eastern North America. Papaws grow to nearly thirteen metres (forty feet) in height and have pointed, broadly oblong drooping leaves up to thirty centimetres (twelve inches) long. In spring they produce an unpleasant-smelling flower about five centimetres (two inches) wide before the leaves appear. The fruits look rather like potatoes, perhaps ten centimetres (about five inches) long, and almost black when they are ripe.

What is bread-fruit?

The fruit of *Artocarpus ineisa*, a tree which grows mainly in Malaya and the South Sea Islands, where it is a staple food; it is round and greenish, weighs a couple of kilogrammes and has a white fibrous pulp, tasting very like bread if baked when not quite ripe.

Bread-fruit was an indirect cause of mutiny on Captain Bligh's ship *Bounty*. She was carrying specimen trees to Jamaica when the crew revolted; and their anger was partly due to the care – and fresh water –

devoted to the saplings over the long voyage, in their special glasshouse on the deck. That batch went overboard when Captain Bligh and the men loyal to him were put off in an open boat, but in 1793 Bligh took another cargo of bread-fruit trees to the West Indies in his new ship *Providence*. A year later George Washington asked for some of them to be brought to the garden of Mount Vernon, his new house on the Potomac in Virginia.

What is an ugli fruit?

It is a cross between a grapefruit and a tangerine, and it *is* ugly – wrinkled and dented, with an unattractive, blotchy skin.

What is a coconut?

Despite its name, it is not a nut but a stone fruit or 'drupe', like a plum. The coconut that you see in a fairground or in the greengrocer's shop is the inner seed or kernel; as it grows it is surrounded by a thick layer of fibre or 'coir' and a woody outer skin. The 'milk' inside the kernel is simply immature or unformed flesh.

Because it has a thick coat of light coconut matting, the coconut fruit floats very easily and is dispersed across oceans by currents and winds. When new islands are thrown up by volcanoes there are usually young coconut palms sprouting on the virgin ground by the time it has cooled enough for man to set foot there.

Coconuts are grown commercially for coconut oil. The dried kernel, now called 'copra', is crushed to extract the oil, which is used for a very wide range of things: for example, soaps and detergents, margarines and cooking fat, synthetic rubber, glycerine, hydraulic-brake fluid and as a plasticizer for safety glass.

To primitive people, the coconut is a genuine tree of life. The kernel provides food and oil for heat and light; the palm leaves are used to build a house; the coir fibre is woven into ropes and mats; and various drugs and wines are made from the root and sap. And all this without mentioning the more obvious examples of carving or burning the wood from the trunk or of making bowls and cups from the shells.

How can cacti survive so long without water?

Cacti are extremely well constructed for survival in dry environments. They have thick-skinned water-retaining stems and extensive root systems; and since they have no leaves – or only very tiny ones – they do not lose water by transpiration like other plants.

The shape of their smooth stems and downward-pointing spines directs any water gathered from dew or the lightest mist directly on to the ground above their roots. And the spines also prevent animals

from climbing the stem to eat the succulent flesh at the top of the cactus.

Almost all cacti occur naturally only on the continent of America, and there are many stories of animals and men surviving long periods in the desert by eating their moist and succulent stems.

Why is grass green?

Because of the chemical, chlorophyll, which is in all plant life and absolutely vital. Without it there could be no life on earth. Chlorophyll absorbs energy from the sun and uses it to convert atoms of oxygen, hydrogen and carbon into the basic plant foods. It also breaks up the molecules of water and carbon dioxide into their various elements and in this process releases oxygen, which we need to breathe. And when cars and factory chimneys belch out deadly gases into the atmosphere, the chlorophyll in grass and in the leaves of trees helps to counteract this poisonous effect.

Why do leaves turn red and yellow in the autumn?

In summer, the red and other colours in the leaf are masked by the green of chlorophyll. When the weather turns colder, and particularly when there is frost, the chlorophyll becomes less active and the other pigments are seen. At the same time a layer of callous cork-like cells grows at the bottom of the leaf's stalk. This cuts off the water and nutrient supply from the plant's roots and makes a breakpoint – so that the leaf eventually falls, either in a high wind or simply under its own weight.

What is yeast?

Yeast is a fungus and like all fungi contains no green cells; so it cannot obtain its food by photosynthesis. Instead it lives on dead matter and is called a 'saprophyte' – after the Greek word *sapros*, meaning rotten.

Yeast is useful to man because it is 'anaerobic'; that is, it does not need air for life. To obtain oxygen it oxidizes sugars into alcohol and carbon dioxide; and it is this carbon dioxide which causes beer to foam, and wine to sparkle and bread to rise.

What makes a nettle sting?

Plants of the botanical family Urticaceae are covered with hollow hairs that have a pointed glass-like tip. These can penetrate the skin at the merest touch – they even go through clothing – and release formic acid when the brittle point breaks off. The result is usually just a burning sensation and a mottled rash that disappears after a few hours. Rubbing the place with a dock leaf does help. The unpleasant reaction is caused by an excess of histamine in the area, and the dock contains the antidote.

But in Australia the tree nettle *Laportea photoniphylla* produces a sting so violent that the victim may run about screaming wildly with pain. And one variety of an American tree nettle, *Urtica holosericea*, is said to have a sting powerful enough to kill a horse.

Oddly enough you can eat the common British stinging nettles, either cooked like spinach or made into a soup. But you must pick them young, wearing gloves, and take only the tender top four leaves of each shoot.

Why do roses have thorns?

It is a defence mechanism to prevent small animals climbing the stems to eat the flowers, and larger ones from eating the stems themselves. Even so, some animals, such as goats, are not deterred. A cow will eat roses too, and so, if it can reach the blooms, will a mouse.

Other plants like the thistle, the blackberry and the holly are protected in a similar way.

What are oak apples?

They are also called button galls, and they are really nothing to do with the oak tree, except that an insect called the gall-wasp, *Biorhiza pallida*, has chosen to make its nest there. It lays its eggs in the end bud of the tree's shoots and the grubs develop in little cells inside the spongy, apple-shaped, reddish-brown growth which results. In July they eat their way out and the oak apples become brown and dry.

Can you really tell the age of a tree by counting its rings?

Yes, you can. Each year, as the tree grows, it produces a layer of large, thin-walled light-coloured cells in the spring and summer with smaller, thick-walled darker cells at the end of the growing season. Then growth stops abruptly when the sap ceases to flow in the autumn. This makes an annual ring round the trunk that is sharply defined by the darker cells at its edge; and the ring's width will vary according to whether the year was a good or bad season.

The oldest living trees are the bristlecone pines of eastern California's White Mountains. Dendrochronologists (people who count the age of trees!) at the University of Arizona estimate that approximately a hundred trees in that forest are older than four thousand years, and that the bristlecone pine could live to five thousand five hundred. However, the oldest they know, named Methuselah, is about four thousand, six hundred years old.

What is mistletoe?

Mistletoe, *viscum album*, is the only woody plant in Britain that grows parasitically on trees. But it does have chlorophyll, and so is only a hemi– (half–) parasite. It obtains nourishment from the parent tree and also converts carbon dioxide, using the energy of light. It grows well on old oak and apple trees whose rough surface provides good crannies in which the 'planted' seed can lodge. Birds like its glutinous white berries – especially, of course, the missel thrush – and they help to distribute the sticky seed by rubbing their beaks against the tree's bark.

What is a bulb?

Plants like tulips, lilies and onions have a resting stage when the food they will need for the next year's growth is preserved in storage places underground. These bulbs consist of a short stem surrounded by fleshy leaves, with a bud at the centre from which the new shoot will come. In tulip bulbs, the stored material is mainly starch; in onions, it is sugar; and it is because of these reserve food supplies that spring bulbs will flower well in plain water or in a relatively weak medium such as peat.

Once the plant has flowered, the surface leaves must remain for some time so that they can gather and store away more energy in the form of buried food supplies. If you cut them off, only a small bulb will form, and a spindly flower next year.

New bulbs develop on top of the last year's one; and they have curious contractile roots that are able to drag the bulb down to the depth of soil it needs.

What is a corm?

Corms are very like bulbs but the food store is in a vertical fleshy stem rather than in the leaf structure. Crocuses, gladioli and montbretia all have corms, and each produces cormels or young corms at the base or side.

Tubers, like potatoes and Jerusalem artichokes, and rhizomes, such as iris and Solomon's Seal, are other examples of underground stem food stores.

Where does rubber come from?

Natural rubber comes mainly from the Para rubber tree, *Hevea brasiliensis*, which grows wild in the jungles of Brazil and in Columbia, Peru and Bolivia; but small quantities are also obtained from the Mexican latex tree *Castilloa elastica*, and the Malayan Gutta Percha tree. The Mexican Indians used latex for waterproof clothing from early times, but rubber remained very scarce and expensive until the late nineteenth century, when an English botanist, Sir Henry Wickham, smuggled some seeds of the Para rubber tree out of Brazil and grew them in the glasshouses of Kew Gardens. Then the great rubber plantations of Sri Lanka, Malaya, India and Indonesia were planted.

Rubber trees need a hot, moist climate and take six or seven years to mature. Then a spiral groove is cut in the bark halfway round the trunk, and the latex flows along this from the living inner bark. It runs into a spout that has been driven into the trunk and then into a collecting cup. The latex seals as it dries so every second or third day a fresh cut has to be made.

After the latex has been collected, lactic acid is added to make it coagulate, and the 'curd' that results is squeezed between rollers to form a sheet. This is then hung in a smokehouse to cure and dry.

During World War II, when the Japanese occupied most of the Far East rubber plantations, synthetic rubbers were developed, using chemical processes. And today more than half the rubber used is manufactured synthetically.

How does sound get on to a record?

Sound causes things to vibrate, each note in a different way; high notes cause more frequent vibrations and loud notes greater ones. Sound to be recorded is picked up by a microphone, which converts its various elements into electric currents. These are transmitted to a sapphire cutting-needle suspended above a soft plastic disc, and the vibrations collected by the microphone are recorded there. The needle wavers as it goes round in a spiral from the edge to the centre of the record; it wavers more frequently for higher sounds and with wider wiggles if the sound is loud. You can see these waves if you look at a gramophone record through a magnifying glass.

Tape recorders or cassette players record the sound on a plastic or paper tape impregnated with iron oxide. Sounds are passed from a microphone to a ring-shaped electromagnet called a head, and at the same time the coated tape is drawn over it. As it passes over the head the tape is magnetized in sympathy with the various sounds. The louder they are the stronger the currents from the mike and the greater the magnetization on the tape.

When the tape is played back the variations of magnetism in it produce similar variations in the iron core of the playing head. This induces different electric currents in the coils around the core which, amplified and fed into a loudspeaker, reproduce the original sound.

Finally, when you are tired of that particular recording, the tape can be run over a third head which contains a high-frequency electric current. This de-magnetizes the tape, erasing the sound on it, and then the tape can be used again.

Where is the world's largest telescope?

There are two kinds of optical telescope: refracting ones which magnify the image by a series of lenses, and reflector ones which use mirrors to collect light.

The largest refracting telescope is nineteen metres (sixty-two feet) long and was finished in 1897 at the Yerkes Observatory at Williams Bay, Wisconsin in the United States.

The biggest reflector telescope is on Mount Semirodriki, near Zelenchukskaya in the Caucasus Mountains of Russia. It was built between 1967 and 1972. The mirror weighs some seventy tonnes and measures six metres (236 inches) across. The light-gathering power of this immense telescope is so great that you could see a candle 24,000 kilometres (15,000 miles) away.

Why do brass instruments play flat when they are cold?

You would think that a brass tuba, for example, would play higher in cold weather because metal contracts in the cold and in general small instruments produce a higher note. And this is in fact the case. Sound is produced by vibrations, the more per second the higher the note, and they are more frequent in a shorter instrument. But this effect is not very great – a five-metre (about sixteen-foot) tuba will only shrink about half a millimetre (0·02 of an inch) at freezing point – and there is another, stronger factor working in the opposite direction: the temperature of the air inside. For pitch is related also to the density of the air through which the vibrations pass. The thinner the air the faster they can go. In a warm room they will travel at 1,230 kilometres (770 miles) per hour, but at only 1,180 kilometres (740 miles) per hour at freezing point. In the same way, if you fill a wind instrument with a light gas such as hydrogen or helium it will produce a higher note.

How fast do you go in free fall?

It is reckoned that the human body reaches 99 per cent of its low-level terminal velocity after falling about six hundred metres (two thousand feet) – which takes about four seconds. This represents about 190 kilometres (120 miles) per hour at normal atmospheric pressure, unless you are travelling head first – when you might get up to 295 kilometres (185 miles) per hour.

In the longest delayed drop, made in August 1960, Captain Joseph W. Kittinger reached speeds of up to 985 kilometres (614 miles) per hour, falling through rarefied air. He left a balloon at 31,150 metres (102,800 feet) and dropped 25,500 metres (84,700 feet) before opening his parachute.

In January 1942 a Russian called I. M. Chrisov fell from his plane without a parachute. He dropped nearly 6,650 metres (22,000 feet) and struck the ground on the edge of a snow-covered ravine, where he slid to the bottom. He survived, though he had a broken pelvis and serious spine damage.

In March 1944 a pilot called Nicholas Alkemade jumped from his blazing Lancaster bomber over Germany without a parachute. He was flying at 5,450 metres (18,000 feet). His fall was arrested by a fir tree and he landed without a broken bone in a snowbank forty-five centimetres (eighteen inches) deep.

What makes jet trails in the sky?

Jets run on energy, produced by burning paraffin, a hydro-carbon which when burnt leaves behind oxides of carbon and oxides of hydrogen – carbon dioxide and H_2O. It is much the same principle as makes us go. We eat carbohydrate and breathe out carbon dioxide and H_2O.

In the high sky, where it is very cold, the water vapour turns instantly into crystals of ice to make a white trail.

What is carbon dating?

Carbon dating or radio-carbon dating is used by archaeologists to estimate the age of ancient objects made of organic matter. They do this by measuring the content of the radioactive isotope, carbon 14. The impact of cosmic rays on the Earth's atmosphere causes a very small proportion of nitrogen atoms to change into atoms of carbon 14, and some of these find their way into living substances.

Carbon 14 has a known 'half life': every 5,730 years the amount contained in an object is halved. Taking the example of a wooden object, we know that the wood could not have added to its store of carbon 14 once the tree was felled; so the age of the object can be reckoned with remarkable accuracy.

What is radar?

Electromagnetic radio waves sent out by a transmitting antenna are interrupted by any object, such as a ship, aeroplane or even a mountain, and a part of the energy is reflected back. The reflection is called an echo; and the reflecting object a target. Echoes from desired targets are known as 'target signals', or simply signals, whereas echoes from other objects, that make it difficult to spot the target, are referred to as 'clutter'.

The distance to a target can be determined absolutely accurately by the time taken for the wave to travel from the transmitter to the target and bounce back, because radio waves move at the speed of light.

Sonar or Asdic systems for underwater detection work on the same principle as radar, using the transmission and reflection of a probe of energy as the basis of their operation. Primitive depth detectors or echo sounders were in use in the 1930s; but during World War II the Americans developed a system that could rapidly scan either a sector of the ocean or all round, using a narrow beam and without having to move the transmitter or the receiver. There were two types of beam: a vertical one bounced off the sea-floor to determine the depth of the target, and the other worked horizontally to locate underwater objects near the surface. The Allies' lead in sonar devices gave them a tremendous advantage over the German Navy.

How are fireworks made?

Fireworks were invented by the ancient Chinese, who used mixtures of saltpetre (potassium nitrate), sulphur and charcoal. They spread to Europe with other explosives during the Middle Ages, when firework displays were often organized by the military technicians of the day. But the colours were always those of ordinary flame until the chemical, potassium chlorate, was introduced in the nineteenth century. It produces so much heat when it burns that a metal burnt with it will turn into gas, which colours the sparks or flame.

There are two main classes of fireworks: force-and-spark and flame. In force-and-spark composition, potassium nitrate, sulphur and

finely-ground charcoal are mixed with various ingredients that produce different types of sparks. They are packed in thick cases strong enough not to burn up; and as a result the pressure set up by the gases throws out a jet of partly consumed material to produce the 'golden rain' or similar effect. Flame mixtures such as the coloured mist effect and also the stars that burst from rockets in the sky are packed in thin cases that are quickly burnt up. They usually contain potassium nitrate, salts of antimony, arsenic or sulphur. For coloured fire, potassium chlorate or potassium perchlorate is combined with a metal salt. Strontium produces red; barium, green; sodium, yellow; and copper, combining with the chlorine gas given off by the potassium chlorate, blue.

One of the most popular forms of firework, the rocket, is lifted into the sky by the recoil produced by the jet of fire thrown out by the chemicals burning in its strong narrow case. It is designed to produce maximum combustion – and so maximum thrust – in its earliest stage.

Fireworks are very dangerous, as the chemicals they contain can produce terrible burns. You should never take liberties with them: never, for example, undo one to see how it is constructed; never carry them around in a pocket; never return to look at one that has been lit to see why it has not gone off. The best firework displays by far are ones that have been organized properly with responsible adults in charge and the onlookers kept apart, where they can enjoy the display in safety.

Why do fabrics shrink?

As it is spun, woven and finished, fabric is subjected to a good deal of pull and stretch, which produce internal stresses in it. When the material gets wet, in a shower of rain or, especially, by washing in hot water, these locked-up stresses are released and the fibres revert to their original length: the cloth shrinks.

Some manufacturers try to reduce the shrinkage by a process called 'Sanforizing'. The material goes through a moistening chamber to soften it. Then it passes over a felt belt where it is firmly pressed by a heated pad. This reduces the amount of tension in the fibres and makes it less likely to shrink.

Man–made fibres such as nylon and polyester do not shrink, though they can sometimes be damaged in other ways by washing or ironing at high temperatures.

What is a breathalyser?

It is a device used by the police to test whether a driver has been drinking. The breathalyser shows roughly how much alcohol is in the breath – and therefore in the bloodstream.

The analysis is done by a photometric colour-meter. A precise amount of air – the driver's breath filling the balloon at the end – passes through a chemical solution of potassium dichromate and sulphuric acid. The colour-density change in the solution is proportional to the amount of alcohol in the sample.

What is radiation?

The same name is given to two things: to the process of emitting electromagnetic energy – such as heat, light, gamma rays, X-rays, subatomic particles, and to the energy or particles that are emitted, or sent out.

Certain kinds of radiation, particularly gamma rays, protons and alpha particles, cause ionization in the substances that they strike. So terms such as 'radiation chemistry', 'radiation biology', 'radiation pathology' and 'radiation physics' have grown up. They refer to the study of the effects of these ionizations on chemical substances, living matter, disease and so forth.

Why does glue stick?

Probably because it holds two items closely together: materials seem to have a natural adhesive power.

Natural glue is a gelatine-like sticky substance extracted from animal tissue such as hides and bones, fish, casein (milk solids) or vegetables. It has been used for at least three thousand years, and though synthetic resin adhesives such as the epoxies are replacing glue for many purposes nowadays, glue is still used in woodwork, in making sandpaper and as a colloid in industrial processes such as the recovery of solid particles suspended in a liquid.

During the 1960s studies were made to try to understand adhesion better, and as a result a new broad theory called the 'adsorption theory' is steadily gaining favour. According to this, two materials will adhere through intimate molecular contact if they are placed close enough together. If they are really close you need no chemical bond. Proponents of this theory point to a universal intermolecular force that holds the solid matter of the world together and claim that adhesion is governed by the same principle of physical adsorption, an attraction mechanism inherent in any surface.

The adsorption theory of adhesion contradicts the popular idea that adhesives must be sticky or tacky. Any material is potentially adhesive. Even plain water can make or cause close molecular contact with a material; it fails to hold only because its sheer strength is low and because it evaporates.

Why do gliders fly?

Gliders have no engine to drive them forward, so they rely on upward air currents to gain height and sustain their flight. Once up, they can glide downwards at an angle determined by the ratio of drag to lift – the drag representing the normal force of gravity and the lift provided by the design of the aircraft and the upward pressure of air on its surfaces, particularly the large wings. They are helped, too, by their very light construction.

Gliders are usually launched by towing them along the runway until their wings lift them into the air. Or they may be pulled into the sky behind an aeroplane or catapulted up with a high-speed winch.

Though it is heavier than air, a glider can rise in the sky if the velocity of a rising air current is greater than the speed of the glider's fall. So the glider pilot needs considerable experience and knowledge of weather conditions. Rising currents of air develop on hillsides, over warm areas of land and under cumulus clouds that are just forming. And there are often good rising currents along fronts between warm and cold air masses such as are found on the edge of a thunderstorm.

What is mercury and where does it come from?

Mercury is the only metal that is liquid at ordinary temperatures; it freezes into a soft metal like tin or lead at approximately $-40°$ centigrade ($-40°$ Fahrenheit). Normally silvery white in colour, it slowly discolours in moist air and mixes readily with most other metals, except iron, to form amalgams. It is very heavy, nearly twice the weight of zinc and a quarter as heavy again as lead. Known as quicksilver nowadays, it was sometimes called liquid silver in ancient times, when it was used by the Chinese and Egyptians as long ago as 1500 BC.

There are some natural deposits of mercury but it mostly occurs in the form of a red sulphide called cinnabar. There are important mines at Almadén in Spain, at Monte Amiata in Italy, in Russia and in California, China and Peru. To extract the mercury, cinnabar is roasted in furnaces. The upper end of the furnace is connected to a system of condensers consisting of a series of linked vertical cast-iron pipes. Here the gaseous mercury condenses and collects in hoppers under a water seal. It is 99·9 per cent pure.

Because mercury does not wet or cling to glass and because of its uniform volume and expansion rate throughout its liquid range, it is immensely valuable for making thermometers and barometers. An electrical discharge through mercury vapour produces a bluish glow rich in ultra-violet light which is used in ultra-violet fluorescent and high-pressure mercury-vapour lamps. And it is used as a shield and coolant in nuclear reactors.

What happens to an empty oil well?

The space usually fills with water naturally, but sometimes the space from which gas or oil have been taken is filled artificially. This counteracts the pressures that build up when the oil or gas is removed, and reduces the risk of subterranean collapse.

Sometimes, when nearly all the gas or oil from a deposit has been drawn off, the pressure inside the well drops so that the mineral will no longer flow. Then water is pumped in under high pressure to try to force the deposit out. If this does not work, the last bit of mineral fuel has to be pumped out.

How does soap work?

To clean things you need to get them wet and to disperse the dirt into the water. Water by itself is not very efficient. Its surface tension, or the attraction its molecules have to one another rather than to the cloth's fibre or the person's skin, prevents it making things really wet. Adding soap or detergent increases the water's spreading and melting ability so that it penetrates. Then a layer of soapy water is absorbed between the material being washed and the dirt on its surface. A good rub with the hands, or agitation from the washing machine, and the dirt floats off.

This is the basic principle, but there are several refinements in modern soaps and washing powders. For example, a 'colloid', or gluey substance, is added to keep the dirt suspended and prevent it floating back on to the cloth. And that whiter-than-white appearance is achieved by optical brighteners. These are taken in by the fibres and convert invisible ultra-violet light into visible light on the blue side of the spectrum. When this is reflected off the fabric the colours look brighter, and yellowed material seems – indeed is – white again. Other additives are 'sequestering agents', which combine with calcium and magnesium ions to make hard water soft, and abrasives such as powdered pumice or talc to give the cleanser extra scouring power.

How is instant coffee made?

There are two ways of doing this.

In the spray-drying method a concentrated brew of coffee is sprayed into a chamber where hot dry air is pumped. The air carries away the moisture, leaving bubble-shaped particles behind.

The other process is freeze-drying. The strong coffee extract is frozen and put into a vacuum chamber where the moisture is 'sublimated' or taken out. This leaves a solid mass which is broken up before packing in tins or jars.

Why is cheese hard?

Because most of the water has been pressed out. If milk is not used within a few days it sours and forms an acid curd made from the chief protein in milk, casein. The clear fluid, whey, runs out and leaves a semi-solid fresh cheese which might be cottage cheese or the Scots 'crowdie'. Harder cheeses like Cheddar or Gouda are pressed again and stored to ripen, and they vary a great deal according to this processing. Cheddar cheese, for example, has butter mixed into it; and moulds are encouraged in blue-veined cheeses like Gorgonzola and Stilton.

About ten times as much milk goes into making half a kilogramme, or a pound, of cheese, and it is very rich in nutrients as well as being a

good way of preserving food for the winter months. There are literally thousands of varieties made from the milk of cows, goats, sheep, water buffaloes, mares, llamas and yaks.

How is glass made?

The raw materials that are used for making glass are the same today as they were in ancient times – sand, soda and limestone or chalk, though the quantities vary and there are different additives according to the kind of ordinary or special glass you want to make. The materials are heated in a furnace until they melt, and the glass is cleared by adding manganese dioxide, antimony oxide and even arsenic.

For coloured glass, metallic oxides such as iron, copper, manganese or chromium are put in. Lead goes into lead crystal – which is brighter and more brittle than ordinary glass – and gold produces a rich ruby colour. Then the thick liquid melted material is formed into the required shapes by casting, rolling, drawing, moulding, blowing, spinning or pressing. This is usually done by machines but, for fine work, hand-forming processes, often involving special blowpipes, are still used. After the glass has been shaped it is very important that it is cooled correctly so that it is kept free from weak stress points.

What is cement?

Ordinary modern cement contains roughly 64 per cent lime, 21 per cent silica, 6 per cent alumina, 3 per cent iron oxide, 2 per cent magnesia, 2 per cent sulphur trioxide and 1 per cent alkalis; but there are variations on these percentages according to the type of cement – modified, low-heat, sulphate-resisting, and so forth.

The Greeks and Romans made cement by blending ground lime with volcanic ash. It was mixed with water and slowly hardened to make either mortar or a kind of concrete. But in the Middle Ages the secret was lost. In 1756 the English engineer John Smeaton was commissioned to build the Eddystone lighthouse off the Devon coast. He needed a material that would harden under water and managed to make a natural cement by grinding up Welsh limestone. Then in 1824 Joseph Aspdin of Leeds took out a patent for a material produced from a synthetic mixture of limestone and clay. He called it Portland Cement because he fancied it resembled Portland stone. It didn't much, but it was certainly hard and excellent for sticking together bricks or stones and for mixing with an aggregate to make concrete.

Cement is made by blending together roughly two-thirds chalk containing lime and roughly one-third clay containing silica or alumina. Water is added and they are ground wet in a washmill to form a slurry which is then burned at a very high temperature – 1,400° to 1,450° centigrade (2,552° to 2,652° Fahrenheit) – to decompose the powdered limestone into lime and carbon dioxide. The lime then combines with the clay to form clinker. 4 per cent gypsum (hydrous calcium sulphate) is added and great ball-mills containing rotating steel balls grind the clinker to a powder that is cement.

Cement must be kept dry until it is used and you cannot work with it when the temperature is below freezing, for then it cannot 'hydrate', or combine with the water, properly.

How does a barometer work?

By atmospheric pressure. It consists of a long tube filled with mercury and turned upside-down in a vessel that contains more mercury. This is pushed down by atmospheric pressure and in turn makes the mercury in the tube rise. Low pressure usually indicates a change in the weather – for air from another place where the pressure is high will rush in, bringing rain and wind with it.

Atmospheric pressure can be expressed in various ways: as pounds per square inch; as dynes per square centimetre (a dyne is $\frac{1}{980}$ of a gramme); or in millibars (one millibar equals 1,000 dynes per square centimetre). Normal atmospheric pressure is about 1·029 kilogrammes per square centimetre (14·7 pounds per square inch) which is equal to 1,013 millibars. It is generally lower at high altitudes than at sea level, and this fact is used in altimeters, which measure height.

What is a nuclear reactor?

It uses nuclear energy in a controlled way to generate power. Although this can be done by both 'nuclear fission' (splitting) and 'nuclear fusion' (joining), nuclear fission has been used in all commercial reactors so far.

The central part of the operation is the 'nuclear pile'. This is a quantity of fissionable material such as uranium which is great enough to create nuclear energy spontaneously. Any 'heavy' element with an atomic number of 84 or more can be used. The aim is to create a 'critical mass', for when you put sufficient fissionable material together fission results. The same force created the atomic bomb, but in a reactor it is controlled.

Fission starts when an atom of uranium is struck by a neutron. The uranium nucleus vibrates, splits into two, and ejects two or three neutrons at high speed. If each of these then strikes another atom of uranium further fission happens, and more and more heat is generated. The productivity is in fact fantastic. If all the atoms in a pound of uranium 235 were to go into fission the result in heat produced would be the equivalent of burning 1,500 tonnes of coal. But the reaction does need to be controlled. This is done by a moderator. Rods made from cadmium or boron, which absorb neutrons readily, are inserted into the reactor to slow down the process, or withdrawn to speed it up.

How does a coral reef form?

Coral consists of millions of tiny skeletons, with the still living coral organisms clinging to the dead. The coral animal is a marine polyp with a cylindrical body. This is attached at the lower end and has a mouth at the other, surrounded by tentacles. The polyp siphons water down into its muscular throat and extracts the algae on which it feeds. As it matures a stony skeleton develops, either externally in a cup-like shape or in the form of tiny spicules inside.

When the coral dies, the skeleton, which is almost pure calcium carbonate, contributes to the reef's growth. The rate varies according to food supply and water temperature but is between 0·5 and 2·8 centimetres (0·2 and 1·1 inches) per year.

Most Pacific islands are coral formations, though they all have a central non-coral core which is usually volcanic. In the shallow waters of the tropics the coral polyp is attracted to the islands' edges. Gradually, partially submerged platforms of limestone are formed with the living coral organisms on the outer ocean edge, for they feed on organisms carried by the waves and currents. Eventually a barrier reef builds up, separated from the shore of the island by a narrow lagoon.

A coral atoll occurs when the original island core subsides, leaving a circle or oval of coral surrounding a lagoon. The ring is usually broken to form a horseshoe shape, its opening on the sheltered or leeward side where there is less waterborne food for the coral to feed on. Within this lagoon a number of islets usually form. They are made of reef debris and may reach six to nine metres (twenty to thirty feet) above sea level. Kwajalein Atoll in the Marshall Islands is the world's largest formation of this kind. It is 283 kilometres (176 miles) long and thirty-two kilometres (twenty miles) wide, with a lagoon area of 2,850 square kilometres (1,100 square miles).

The island of Guam has another impressive coral formation. There, the land has risen over the centuries and ancient coral reefs are now limestone cliffs about 180 metres (600 feet) high.

Why is the sea salty?

The salt is carried there by the rivers, which dissolve all sorts of minerals into their waters as they cut across the land surfaces and eventually deposit them into the seas. The result is so much salt in the oceans of the world that if they all dried up enough would remain to cover the world's land surfaces to a depth of about sixty metres (200 feet).

The degree of salinity of sea water varies a great deal. In hot places, where there is high evaporation, the solution is more concentrated, while greater rainfall dilutes the oceans of the north. The average level for all sea waters is 3·7 per cent, but in the Gulf of Bothnia in the Baltic the percentage of salt is only 0·1, while in the Dead Sea it is over 25 per cent, making the water so buoyant you can sit in it to read a newspaper.

The salinity of the world's oceans stays fairly steady. The seas are constantly added to by rivers, glaciers, rainwash and volcanic action; but water plants and creatures are taking minerals out at the same time. And minerals are also lost in deposits of limestone and salts in shallow lagoons and salt pans along the shoreline.

What are quicksands?

They are 'quick' in the old biblical sense of 'alive' – as in the phrase 'the quick and the dead'; and they consist of sand that has become so saturated with water it has lost its capacity to hold things up. They

73

often occur near the mouths of large rivers and may be caused by a bowl-shaped underlayer of clay or rock through which water cannot drain away. Sometimes, however, the quicksands are formed by the agitation of strong currents and tides; and in that case the sands may be 'quick' only under certain conditions. The dreaded Goodwin Sands off Dover are of this sort.

Although quicksands have certainly caused many deaths, the density of the sand-and-water mixture is higher than that of the human body; it should give enough support to hold at least your nose and mouth up in the air. So if you should be caught in a quicksand, don't struggle; it only digs you in deeper and can cause death. It is far better to stay still and shout for help.

What is sand?

It is mineral, rock or soil particles that range in diameter from 0·06 to two millimetres (0·0024 to 0·08 inches). Much of it is quartz but most of the rock-forming minerals that occur on the earth's surface are found in sand, and in some areas there are quantities of feldspar, chalk, iron ores and volcanic glass. Most quartzose sands contain some feldspar and also small plates of white mica which, although it is soft, decomposes only slowly.

All sands contain small amounts of heavy rock-forming minerals, such as garnet, zircon, topaz, pyroxenes and so forth. In some shore and river areas the action of the currents and tides concentrates these heavier particles and it is then possible to sift and wash the sand to retrieve deposits of precious stones, gold, platinum and tin. Greensands, which are widely distributed over the ocean floor and are also found in ancient strata on the continents, owe their colour to the presence of glauconite, a mineral that contains potash; it is used for softening water.

Very pure quartzose sands are used in pottery and glassmaking as a source of silica, and similar sand is needed for lining the hearths of acid-steel furnaces. The sands used in foundries for making the moulds in which the metal is cast usually have a clay content to unite the grains so that the mould holds its shape. Quartz and garnet sands are used in abrasives; and ordinary sands find a multitude of uses in construction – sand is needed for everything built with mortar or concrete.

What is a fossil?

It is either the remains of a plant or animal or just the outline preserved in the earth's crust. This usually happens only when the living thing was buried quickly to prevent decomposition or destruction by scavengers and when it had hard parts capable of being fossilized in the first place. But soft parts might have been saved by freezing. A good example of this is the preservation of mammoths in ice, though most fossils are quite small. Fossilized hard parts, such as the shells of clams or brachiopods are fairly common in sedimentary rocks and many of them are very old.

Even fossils with hard parts often survive only in an altered form. Shells and bones are frequently 'permineralized' – that is, made denser by the addition of mineral matter such as calcium carbonate or even various iron materials taken in from the surrounding rock or soil. The original crystal structure of a shell may be recrystallized or even replaced by pyrite, hematite or silica, while its external appearance remains unaltered. Moulds or casts of structures are also common; they form when the original material is dissolved away and the resulting spaces are filled by tightly packed particles of sediment. Traces of organisms also occur as tracks or trails, even borings, made by the living creature.

Fossils tell an enormous amount about the age of the rock formations in which they are found, the type of plant and animal life that lived there and the way in which it died.

What makes an emerald green?

There is a trace of chromic oxide, Cr_2O_3, in the basic beryllium aluminium silicate. Other variations in colour are caused by additional traces of iron and vanadium. Most of the finest emeralds come from South America – Colombia and Brazil – but they are also found in the Ural Mountains and in New South Wales.

Emeralds are the most valuable of all the gem stones. This is partly because they are very brittle, so uncracked crystals are rare. And they keep their colour in artificial light.

How large do sea waves get?

The highest wave officially recorded was measured aboard the USS *Ramapo* on a voyage from the Philippines to San Diego in California. During a gale early in February 1933 a wave was computed to be over thirty-three metres (110 feet) from its trough to its crest.

The highest wave precisely measured on instruments was twenty-four metres (seventy-seven feet). This was recorded by the British weather ship *Weatheradviser* when she was on station in the North Atlantic early in 1968.

Why does water expand when it is turned into ice?

It is just a simple physical fact: water has the property of being less dense when in its solid state. So a given amount of water takes up more space when you freeze it.

As the ice is less dense, it has more buoyancy, and floats on the surface of the denser water below. But they both have the same chemical formula: H_2O.

How are glaciers formed?

When a layer of ice resting on a slope has built up to a depth of ninety metres (three hundred feet) or more, the deeper part behaves as if it were a highly viscous liquid. Gradually it yields and flows down the slope, carrying the rigid upper crust with it. Crevasses occur when the land beneath is suddenly steeper; the crust cracks as the ice beneath slips away.

Glaciers only form when more snow falls, year in, year out, than is lost by melting and evaporation. Freshly fallen snow has a very low density – as much as 90 per cent of its volume may be air-filled pockets – but changes set in quickly as it packs down. The hexagonal (six-sided) snow crystals change into more rounded, smaller particles; and air vents make up less than 50 per cent of the volume in this old granular snow. Then, as it compacts even further, the old snow reaches a point where it may be called 'firn', or névé, with a density about four-tenths that of water. Snow still falls on top, compacting the 'firn' to glacial ice. Some air remains trapped even at this point: the ice-density is now roughly five-sixths that of water.

Glaciers are found mostly in areas of high mountains and plateaux. There, the yearly average temperatures are low, and mountains often receive heavy snowfall. There are glaciers in equatorial latitudes, though usually only well above 4,500 metres (15,000 feet); and in the cold climates of Arctic regions glaciers form at low elevations and run down to sea level. Windward coasts encourage their formation because the moisture-laden air from the sea causes heavy falls of snow, particularly on the west coasts of continents in the middle-to-high latitudes. But mountains lying far in the continental interiors generally do not receive the heavy snowfall that glaciers need.

What causes an avalanche of snow?

Named from the French dialect word *avalance* meaning 'descent', an avalanche is a sudden slide or slip of snow. There are two main types: the grand avalanche of wet snow and ice, which slides over the ground and carries with it quantities of earth, stone and other debris; and the powder avalanche, which consists of dry powdery snow that flies up into the air in great clouds as the avalanche comes down.

The avalanche happens when a mass of snow which has been pent up on a mountainside loses its hold and rushes down. Wet snow has been known to avalanche on a slope of only 15°, while hard snow that has lain for a long time and been packed down often remains on slopes as steep as 50°.

Irregularities in the ground such as rocks or mounds act as anchoring points and help to arrest any tendency to avalanche; and bushes and trees standing close together also help to hold the snow back. Another important factor is the structure of the snow. Most avalanches start in the upper layers of snow which are not weighted down by more snow on top. In some places, this dry powdery mass is so delicately balanced that the vibration of a gunshot or even a loud shout will make it hurtle down. Climbers and skiers go very quietly in these areas, and they also wear long avalanche ropes which trail behind them. Then if one of them should be overcome, the rescue party would know where to dig for the buried person.

What are geysers?

The word geyser, meaning 'spouter' or 'gusher', comes from the Icelandic *geysir*. It is a hot spring from which water and steam are expelled vigorously and intermittently. Geysers are rarer than hot springs but they tend to occur in the same areas, and are caused by volcanic activity in the hot molten material beneath the crust of the Earth.

In Iceland, geysers and hot springs cover an area of about 130,000 square kilometres (50,000 square miles). The Great Geyser of this region is particularly well known, and although it is diminishing in flow it still sends up a daily jet of water nearly sixty metres (two hundred feet) high and three metres (ten feet) in diameter that lasts for twenty minutes.

In the Yellowstone Park area of the United States there are some two hundred geysers, besides three thousand or more hot springs, steam vents and 'paint pots'. Here tiny geysers erupt every few minutes while giant ones, some with descriptive names like 'the

Giantess', 'the Castle' and 'the Beehive', send out enough hot water to supply a small town.

The largest geyser was at Waimauku in New Zealand. It appeared in 1901 and was active for about two years. At its peak it spouted a column of water 455 metres (1,500 feet) high, and once threw a rock weighing 68 kilogrammes (150 pounds) half a kilometre (a quarter of a mile).

Does bathwater always run away in the same direction?

Yes it does, at least in theory. Because of the Coriolis forces produced by the rotation of the Earth, water swirls anti-clockwise in the Northern Hemisphere and clockwise in the Southern. This has been demonstrated in Boston, Massachusetts, and in Sydney, Australia. But you may not get the right result in your bathtub experiment because the Coriolis effect is so weak that it can easily be over-ruled by other stronger velocities. So let the water settle, make sure it is of even temperature, and check that there are no currents of air in the room. Then pull out the plug as gently as you can.

Why doesn't a ship sink?

It is because of buoyancy. Liquids have a natural upthrust or holding power which varies according to their weight. When a solid object is immersed in water the buoyancy equals the weight of the water displaced, which is also the same as the object's weight.

Since a ship is hollow – unlike a log of wood – it has a relatively high natural buoyancy; and in addition there is the reserve buoyancy of the watertight area above the waterline – the level at which the vessel floats. This extra hollow area, called the 'freeboard', allows the ship to survive some flooding if it is damaged below sea level, as well as the tossing of a storm.

What is electricity?

It is the movement of electrons from a place that is negatively charged to one that is positively charged. Every atom contains electrons (which are negatively charged) and protons (positively charged). Negative and positive always attract each other, while two things charged the same way, negatively or positively, push each other away. Sometimes, when you comb your hair, the friction causes electrons to pass through your hair into the comb. Your hair becomes positively charged, the comb negatively. So your hair stands on end, attracted to the comb. The same energy can be produced by the power of a magnetic field or by burning oil or coal or harnessing hydro- (water-) power.

Some materials, such as copper, allow electrons to move easily along them: they are known as conductors and are used, for example, for electric wiring. Materials that will not allow electricity to pass, such as rubber or plastic, are called insulators.

What causes lightning?

It is a natural electrical discharge that usually happens when the atmosphere contains too much water, though lightning can occur in dust- and snow-storms or in the erupting gas of an active volcano.

When the water-drops in the air become very large they tend to split up into large and small droplets. The larger ones carry a negative electric charge and the smaller a positive one. As the storm proceeds the small droplets are held up in the thunder-clouds while the large ones fall as rain. But positive and negative charges attract each other and, when they are separated, try to get together again. With more rain and more small droplets in the clouds the separate charges build up until the two electric forces become so strong the air between them can no longer hold them apart. The flash starts on the ground and darts upwards into the sky.

What makes it thunder?

When lightning flashes the electric force punctures the atmosphere. The air is torn by the spark and heated rapidly so that it expands at supersonic speed. This shockwave is transmitted to our ears as sound.

The whole length of the channel that lightning cuts produces sound, and it rises upwards from the ground. If you are standing near the place of the lightning strike you hear the noise of a sharp thunderclap followed by a long rumble. Farther away there is less of a clap and more of a rumble or roll. This is because the air between modifies the sound.

Light travels at 298,000 kilometres (186,000 miles) per second, while sound only manages 334 metres (1,100 feet) in that time and is widely dispersed by the air as it goes. So if the lightning strike is more than twenty-four kilometres (fifteen miles) away, no thunder is heard at all. Nearer, the difference between the travelling times of light and sound means that you can work out the distance of the strike. A thunderclap heard two seconds after the lightning flashes means that it was approximately 610 metres (2,000 feet) away. You can estimate the height of the lightning spark in the same way, by the length of the thunder's rumble. If it lasts ten seconds the spark must have been approximately 3,350 metres (11,000 feet) long.

What is the sound barrier?

It is an invisible barrier which occurs when there is a sharp rise in aerodynamic drag when an object – such as an aircraft – approaches the speed of sound. Sonic speed is approximately 1,220 kilometres

(760 miles) per hour. All the time an aircraft is flying slower than 1,220 kilometres per hour the pressure waves (sound waves) it creates can outspeed their sources and spread out ahead. But once the craft reaches sonic speed the waves are unable to get out of its way. Strong local shockwaves form on the wings and body; airflow around the craft becomes unsteady and severe buffeting may result. There can be serious stability difficulties and loss of flight characteristics. This can be very dangerous in aeroplanes designed to operate at just subsonic speeds, but planes properly designed for supersonic flight pass through the sound barrier quite easily.

Why is the sky blue?

It is because of scattered light – a principle discovered by Baron Rayleigh towards the end of the nineteenth century.

The wavelengths of all the different coloured elements of light are very easily deflected by the particles in the atmosphere. But blue light, at the short wavelength end of the spectrum, is the most easily deflected. So on a sunny day the red light at the long end of the spectrum passes on more or less undisturbed and the violet and indigo are largely absorbed; but the blue part of the sun's rays is reflected by the dust and gases of the atmosphere, and it is the blue light that we see.

When the sun sinks in the evening its light has to travel farther and at a greater angle. The blue and green rays are almost all absorbed on the way, while the longer red and yellow rays are able to reach our eyes.

How far away is the horizon?

The distance is regulated by the curvature or roundness of the Earth. It is the boundary where the sky seems to meet the ground or sea.

The higher the observer's eye, the lower and more distant is his visible horizon. If one is looking from 1·5 metres (five feet) above sea level, the horizon is about 3·7 kilometres (2·3 miles) away. But from three metres (ten feet) high, the distance would be about 5·9 kilometres (3·7 miles). At just over 3,000 metres (10,000 feet) the horizon is about 163 kilometres (101 miles).

In fact, on Earth the distance to the horizon in statute miles always equals 0·6395 times the square root of the height in feet above sea level of the observer's eye. On larger or smaller planets the formula varies. On the moon, for example, a man looking from 1·5 metres (five feet) sees a horizon that is only 2·25 kilometres (1·4 miles) from his viewpoint – because the moon is smaller than the Earth.

What is a volcano?

It is a vent or opening in the Earth's crust through which 'magma' – a molten material from inside the Earth – has forced its way to the surface.

The emissions of magma (eruptions) often shape the volcano into the form of a conical mountain, as over the years the erupting materials cool and are deposited thickly around the mouth of the vent.

Further eruptions take place at the top or through the sides of the cone, wherever there is a weak place. Sometimes steam pressure builds up when water percolating through the ground meets the hot magma. This happens particularly if the volcano is near the sea. In 1883 there were dramatic explosions at Krakatoa in the East Indies because cold sea water flowed into the hollow of the molten core. They were so powerful that they blew away the whole island mountain and were heard nearly 5,000 kilometres (3,000 miles) away. Eruptions may also be triggered off by the small movements of the Earth.

Volcanoes are described as active, dormant or extinct – but this is a fairly arbitrary distinction. The ones called dormant simply have not erupted for some time, say a hundred years or more. The active ones erupt in three broadly different ways. In some, the outflow takes place quietly and probably over a large area. A typical volcano of this type is Mauna Loa on the island of Hawaii. Then some erupt explosively every now and then, like Vesuvius in southern Italy, which completely destroyed the Roman city of Pompeii in AD 79. Finally, there are explosive volcanoes of immense violence. Mount Pelée on the island of Martinique was one of these. At the turn of the century it erupted with such energy that it destroyed the city of St Pierre and most of the inhabitants.

Volcanoes are situated along the lines of weakness in the Earth's crust and are most common around the Pacific basin. Here there is a chain of active and recently extinct volcanoes along the eastern edge of Australasia and Asia and continuing down the western side of North and South America. Almost all Pacific islands consist of coral built on to an original volcanic core; and if you take the story even farther back into prehistory, you can argue that most land on Earth is due to volcanic action of some kind. Volcanoes have also contributed greatly to the gases and dust particles that make up the Earth's atmosphere.

What is a tidal wave?

First of all it is nothing to do with the tide. Tidal waves are created by an earthquake under the water, a landslide on the coast or a volcanic eruption. The Japanese name for them is *tsunami*, meaning 'harbour wave', and scientists now call them 'tsunami' to avoid confusion.

The earthquake, landslide or eruption generates a series of oscillatory or pendulum-like waves that radiate out in ever-widening circles, very like the waves produced by a stone thrown into a pond. These seismic waves are very long, perhaps a hundred or even two hundred kilometres (sixty or 125 miles), but they are only a third or two-thirds of a metre (one or two feet) high, and because of their great length and low height they are very difficult to detect on the surface of the ocean among all the other smaller surface waves. A ship may pass over one and not report anything out of the ordinary.

But when the seismic waves approach the coast, friction against the shallow sea-bed reduces the speed. The length of the wave becomes shorter and its height increases to as much as thirty metres (a hundred feet) in a matter of minutes. So when it reaches land the wave may do appalling damage.

Seismic sea waves are reflected and refracted by nearshore bottom topography and coastal configuration. So their effects vary widely from place to place. Occasionally the first sign of a seismic wave's arrival may be a trough, the water receding and exposing the shallow sea-floor. This happened at Lisbon in November 1755. Many people

were attracted out to explore the bay floor – and were drowned moments later by the inrush of water. The underwater eruption that caused this disaster was so powerful that small tidal waves were set up as far north as Loch Ness, and in Loch Lomond the water rose about seventy centimetres (two foot four), then fell, and continued to rise and fall for an hour and a half. In 1703 in Awa, Japan, a seismic wave killed more than a hundred thousand people. And when Krakatoa exploded in August 1883 it created waves as high as thirty-three metres (110 feet) killing more than thirty-six thousand people in the East Indies.

Why are the continents of the Earth shaped the way they are?

There are three main theories about how the great oceans and land masses came about. And each one takes account of the fact that the continents are still shifting, shrinking and growing – but only by relatively small amounts.

At first people believed that as the Earth cooled down many aeons ago the outer crust became too big for the shrinking interior. So, the rocks were crushed together to form high mountains and land masses, like the wrinkles on a withered apple. Certainly, mountain ranges tend to fall in lines and look as if they could have been formed in this way.

Then it was noticed that parts of certain countries and continents seem to fit into the ocean areas of others nearby like the pieces of a rough jigsaw. This led to the theory of 'continental drift'. It was thought that the Earth's surface floated on a layer of viscous or sticky magma and had been bumped up or broken down in many places to form the lands and seas.

In recent years a new idea called 'plate tectonics' has been developed. It accepts the idea that the Earth has a strong brittle crust or 'lithosphere' over a soft yielding layer, the 'asthenosphere', but argues that the crust is made up of six rigid plates which have been deformed as they moved about. The plates, which run under the sea as well as forming the land masses, move sideways and may slide along one another when they meet or clash together to throw up a ridge; and they also rotate. The great Alpine and Himalayan mountain ranges were probably formed by the meeting of the Eurasian, African and Indian plates, while the Eurasian and African plates meet the American one under the sea to form the mid-Atlantic ridge. Deep-sea cores taken from the bed of the Pacific Ocean in 1970 proved that the western part of the Pacific plate has the most ancient oceanic crust of all, dating from the early Cretaceous or upper Jurassic period, 125 to 150 million years ago.

Plate margins tend to be areas of seismic activity and probably account for most of the earthquakes of the world.

What causes earthquakes?

They can originate in various ways, but one principal cause is responsible for all large earthquakes and most small ones. This is the fracturing of rocks in the outer part of the Earth's crust as strain accumulates during geological processes. The breaks occur when the strain reaches a point greater than the rocks' strength, and there are established lines and surfaces of weakness which are active geological faults. The San Andreas fault in California is one example.

Fractures usually start about sixteen to thirty kilometres (ten or twenty miles) beneath the Earth's crust, sometimes even deeper; and in large earthquakes the fracture extends up to the surface so that you can see the displacement between the two sides. It can be vertical or horizontal, or even both.

The force behind this distortion and faulting is the same one that warped and broke the Earth's crust during geological times to produce mountain ranges and ocean basins. It is probably caused by the flow of heat within the Earth, transferring material by convection: a slow but inexorable motion bringing about geological change.

The latest and most fruitful development in understanding Earth-crust movement is called 'new global tectonics', described in the previous question. Certainly most serious earthquakes do seem to occur on the various lines where the six plates of global tectonics meet.

Why do we have four seasons?

They divide the year according to consistent annual changes in the weather. In the Northern Hemisphere winter, spring, summer and autumn begin officially at: the winter solstice, 22-23 December; the vernal equinox, 20-21 March; the summer solstice, 21-22 June; and the autumnal equinox, 22-23 September. (At each equinox the days and nights are equal in length; at the winter solstice the day is the year's shortest; and at the summer solstice the day is the year's longest.) In the Southern Hemisphere all the seasons are reversed.

The change in temperature between summer and winter is caused by a variation in the angle at which the sun's rays reach the Earth's surface and by the difference in duration of sunlight on the Earth. As the Earth moves in its orbit round the sun, its axis stays almost constant at an angle of about $66\frac{1}{2}°$ to the orbital plane. So during the half of each orbit when the North Pole is inclined towards the sun, the Northern Hemisphere receives the sun's rays at an angle closer to $90°$ than the Southern Hemisphere does, leading to warmer days in the north. Six months later the same will be true of the Southern Hemisphere: so the seasons are reversed.

In polar latitudes the year really has only two seasons: a short summer with almost continuous daylight, and a long winter when it is always dark. And in areas close to the equator the difference in solar radiation at various times of the year is very slight. Seasonal weather variations are based largely on rainy and dry periods which result from the movements of the inter-tropical convergence zone, a narrow belt of abundant rainfall that encircles the Earth near the equator. It shifts north and south seasonally with the sun and causes alternate wet and dry seasons in the areas it crosses. Since regions very near the equator are crossed by this belt twice each year, they tend to have two wet and two dry spells while those farther out have one of each every year.

What makes the tides ebb and flow?

Tides are caused by the gravitational pull of the moon and sun; but because the moon is nearer to us its influence is the stronger. All sorts of factors such as the shape of the coastline tend to alter the timing of the tide, but in general high tides occur every twelve hours, twenty-five minutes – half the time the moon apparently takes to go round in the sky. So, high and low tides are roughly one hour later every day.

The difference in height between high and low water varies from day to day according to the phase of the moon. The highest level, known as the spring tide, is reached when the moon is full; the lowest, or neap tide, when the moon is new or very old.

Heights of tides vary enormously. In the Mediterranean and the Baltic Sea the range is very small, but in the Bay of Fundy in Nova Scotia the tide can rise as much as fifteen metres (fifty feet). Many people have suggested harnessing this tremendous free power.

This could be done fairly simply if a barrage were built to close off an estuary or bay. As the tide rose, water would pour in through sluices and could be released through turbines to generate electricity. A more complicated scheme would make the incoming water pass through turbines as well. But unfortunately there are problems: most suitable places where tides are powerful and high are near commercial seaports, and scientists fear that new barrage might cause serious silting. And these huge projects are so expensive to build it is still cheaper to produce electricity from coal. However, studies are being made in Wales, Spain, Germany, Brazil, New Zealand, Russia and India; and at Rance in Brittany a full-scale experimental scheme is actually being built. It should provide 554 million kilowatts of electricity a year.

Under extreme conditions tides can cause terrible damage. In

February 1953 great waves invaded Holland and parts of the North Sea coasts of Britain and Belgium. Half of Holland's land was covered, 1,800 people died, 50,000 cattle drowned and more than 50,000 people lost their homes. The disaster was caused by an unusually high tide that happened to coincide with gales from the north of more than 160 kilometres (a hundred miles) an hour.

Where does the wind come from?

There are two main causes for the movement of air, though many more local factors also influence the wind. At the equator, heat rises all the time and is replaced by colder air sucked in; and the rotation of the Earth causes movement to the right in the Northern Hemisphere and to the left in the Southern. As a result we get the sub-tropical trade winds: north-easterly in the Northern Hemisphere and south-easterly in the Southern. Between them is the equatorial belt of low pressure known as 'the doldrums', where the winds are light and infrequent with long periods of calm. Farther out towards the poles the winds tend to be westerly, particularly in the Southern Hemisphere, where there is only slight disturbance from land masses, and over the North Atlantic.

But local influences constantly over-ride these general trends. Because water retains heat longer than land, the wind at the coast

tends to blow off the sea in the morning and from the land in the evening. Slope winds occur as a downward movement of air into valleys, especially where they have been subjected to radiational cooling on clear nights. The slopes become warm during the day but at night cool more quickly than the free air. Since cold air tends to fall, a local system of slope winds develops with an upslope wind during the day and a downslope wind at night. Near mountains these winds blow down ridges and through gaps and often have local names like 'föhn' or 'mistral'. Other local-named winds are the 'monsoon' which brings moisture from the Indian Ocean to parts of Asia from June to September, the 'sirocco' in Italy which is both a dry wind from the Sahara in summer and a warm sultry one in the winter months, and the 'chinook' on the eastern side of the Rockies.

What is the mistral?

The mistral, or *maestrale*, is a cold, dry, strong wind that occurs in southern France. It blows down from the north along the Lower Rhône Valley, continuously – often for several days at a time. It reaches speeds of more than 100 kilometres (about sixty miles) per hour, and a height of up to three kilometres (about two miles). In winter and spring, when it is most frequent, it sometimes causes considerable damage to crops.

The southward airflow is caused by a high-pressure centre over central France and a low-pressure centre over the north-western Mediterranean, and the velocity of the wind is intensified as it comes down from the highlands to the coast and by the 'jet effect' that results from it being tunnelled through the narrow Rhône Valley.

What is an echo?

An echo is a repetition of sound caused by reflection of sound waves. You can hear them in tunnels and in caves and among mountains, where striking auditory effects are sometimes produced by echoes bouncing back from several reflecting surfaces. In concert halls and theatres they can be a real problem; acoustic engineers try to prevent them when designing the original building, or to eliminate them by all sorts of devices suspended from the ceiling.

In Greek mythology, Echo was a mountain nymph. One day she offended the goddess Hera by keeping her talking and preventing her spying on one of the mistresses of Hera's husband Zeus. As a punishment for this, Echo's power of speech was taken away, except for the ability to repeat another person's last words. Then a hopeless love for Narcissus, who loved only his own reflection, made Echo fade away so that only her voice was left.

What are clouds?

Clouds are formed when air containing water vapour rises. It expands and cools in the upper atmosphere where the pressure is low until eventually the air is saturated with water. The excess vapour then condenses on to airborne particles such as dust or salt nuclei. The concentration of these solid particles in the atmosphere varies from fewer than one hundred particles per cubic centimetre in very clean air to as many as one million particles per cubic centimetre in the dirty air of an industrial city. So it really is true that the sky is more overcast where man has polluted the air. Even so, salt thrown up on the crests of waves in the sea is the most efficient agent for condensation, and the water vapour is also attracted by smoke from forest fires, the exhaust of aeroplanes, and windblown dust from dry areas of land.

Once condensed, the tiny water-droplets are too light to fall. Only 0·01 millimetre in diameter, they have a falling speed of twenty-five millimetres per second, while the updraughts range from a few centimetres to several metres per second. But the larger cloud droplets tend to form in the higher, colder areas of cloud, then drop through the cloud area to fuse with smaller droplets below. The process goes slowly until the droplet has achieved a radius of about thirty micrometres and then quite quickly until it reaches raindrop size.

On the other hand, droplets in the cold upper reaches of a cloud may be supercooled and crystallize as water vapour is sublimated into ice. The ice crystals grow much more rapidly than would water-droplets under the same conditions: crystals can grow to several millimetres across in about ten minutes. Crystals that collide join together to produce a snowflake, which may melt as it descends, to fall as rain or slush, or may reach the ground as snow.

Hail is frozen raindrops. It usually happens in summer storms and is caused by rising air-currents created by heat rising off the land. The rising air lifts raindrops almost ready to fall, up again into the higher, colder layers of the atmosphere. There the raindrops freeze and fuse together. The lumps of ice may fall and rise several times, each time receiving a fresh coating of water which freezes to increase their size. As a result, hailstones have been recorded seven to ten centimetres (three to four inches) in diameter and up to half a kilogramme (about a pound) in weight. Even larger ones may fall to the ground, but they usually consist of several hailstones that have fused together.

What is dew?

It is condensed water vapour; which forms on clear nights when the air is calm or the wind is light. As the temperature drops, exposed surfaces lose heat to the atmosphere by radiation, and since grass blades, leaves, petals and so forth radiate heat more efficiently than air, they become colder than the atmoshhere around them. So the cold surface cools the air nearby and the water vapour in the atmosphere condenses out.

If the surface temperature is below freezing point hoar frost forms instead.

What is fog?

It is just like a cloud, but near the Earth instead of high above. It is caused by minute particles of water suspended in the atmosphere. Technically, horizontal visibility must be restricted to less than one kilometre (0·62 of a mile) for it to be properly called a fog. If visibility is restricted but you can still see things a kilometre away, the condition is known as a mist or haze. A suspension of ice particles is an ice mist or ice fog.

Fogs happen when the relative humidity of the air becomes high enough for water vapour to condense on nuclei such as particles of dust suspended in the air. The humidity may be due to sudden cooling of moist air or because water vapour has increased rapidly – perhaps by evaporation on a bright day.

Where does dust come from?

Dust consists of trillions of particles so small that you would need about a quarter of a million of them placed side by side to make a line twenty-five millimetres (about an inch) long.

Most natural atmospheric dust comes from the Earth's surface. Smoke from grass and forest fires is an important source. Winds blowing over dry land or deserts raise mineral particles thousands of metres into the air. Erupting volcanoes contribute dust clouds that travel across the world before settling. And meteoroids that vaporize upon entering the upper atmosphere create countless solid particles that eventually descend.

So there is no chance of our ever being able to put away the duster and the carpet sweeper for good: new dust is being introduced into the atmosphere all the time.

What is energy?

The word comes from the Greek *ergon*, meaning 'work', and it is simplest to define energy as the capacity to do work. Physicists use the term 'erg' to count units of energy.

Energy can either be associated with a material object, like a coiled spring or a pendulum; or it can be independent of matter – light and other electromagnetic radiation traversing a vacuum. The important thing is that it carries out work; and you need as much energy to move a heavy object, say, a kilometre, as you need to move something half that weight twice the distance. But a lot of energy is wasted. In machines a great deal is lost by friction, and – the greatest waste of all – we make use on Earth of only a tiny fraction of the power of the sun's rays.

What is a rainbow?

A rainbow is a series of coloured arcs that is seen when light falls upon a collection of water-drops such as rain, spray or fog. The most common rainbows happen when the sun shines upon rain falling in a distant shower. It is always opposite the sun.

The rainbow colours are those of the spectrum: red, orange, yellow, green, blue, indigo and violet. The arc is caused by refraction or bending of light rays that enter the water-drop, each colour resulting from a slightly different angle to the bend. The most brilliant and most common rainbow is the one called the primary bow, which results from light emerging from the water-droplet after one internal reflection. This type of rainbow has an angular radius of about 42°, with the violet-blue arc on the inside and the red-orange outermost.

Sometimes one can see a secondary rainbow. It will be much less intense in colour because it results from light that has undergone two internal reflections within the water-drop. The angular radius of a secondary bow is about 54°, so it appears outside the primary bow and has the colour sequence reversed with violet on the outer arc. Higher-order rainbows, resulting from three or more reflections, are so weak that one can very rarely see them. But sometimes faint circles can be seen within the original half-circle. These are caused by interference bending the light rays as they emerge from the arc, and are called supernumerary rainbows.

Why is the desert hot in the daytime and cold at night?

Many desert regions are relatively high in altitude, so although the ground absorbs a great deal of energy while the sun shines for an average of ten hours a day, it cools again rapidly when night falls. Unlike water, air cannot hold heat for long and its temperature drops almost at once when the heat from the sun has gone. Then the hot ground starts to radiate its heat back into the air. The process is so extreme that the difference in temperature can be as much as 21° centigrade (70° Fahrenheit), and in winter sub-tropical desert areas may have ground frost.

What causes a mirage?

The refraction of light in layers of air that have different densities.

Under some conditions, such as over a stretch of road or in desert air heated by intense sunshine, the air cools rapidly as it rises and at the same time increases in density and refractive power. Sunlight reflected downwards from the top of an object – perhaps a tree – curves up again when it reaches the thin or rarefied air near the ground. The observer sees the object reversed, as if reflected in water, as well as the upright image which travels in a straight line in the normal way. When the image of the sky is refracted the land seems to be a lake or a sheet of water.

Sometimes over water a cool dense layer of air underlies a thin heated one. Then light rays that were originally directed above the line of sight can bend to reach the observer's eye. Something, such as a coastline, that would normally be out of view, is apparently lifted into the sky. This is called 'looming'.

When you drop something, why does it fall?

It is because of gravity, a universal force by which all matter attracts other matter towards itself. Because the Earth is so large (relatively speaking), things tend to fall down towards it, but the gravitational pull of the moon and sun creates the tides of the Earth's waters; and even a large mountain will exert a small sideways gravitational force.

Because of its long reach and universal application, gravity plays a central part in the structure and evolution of stars, galaxies, and in fact the entire universe. It determines the trajectories of celestial bodies and allows planets such as Earth and Mars to retain their atmosphere.

The theory of gravity was at least partly understood by the second-century Greek mathematician Ptolemy, and Galileo did some valuable experiments on the way things fall. But the actual law is always referred to as Newton's Law, after the seventeenth-century British scientist, Sir Isaac Newton. It is sometimes said that he first began to think about the problem when an apple fell from a tree and narrowly missed his head.

Why doesn't the Earth's atmosphere escape into space?

Earth attracts all matter within its gravitational field, even the air which we think of as having almost no weight. Molecules of the atmospheric gases are attracted Earthward and tend to crowd together progressively, becoming more and more dense from the outer limits of the atmosphere down to sea level as each layer is compressed by the weight of the one above it. As a result, any surface exposed to this atmospheric pressure, such as the top of your head, is under a force represented by the weight above, of roughly one kilogramme per square centimetre (fourteen pounds per square inch). The force of atmospheric pressure varies according to the distance from the centre of the Earth; at the top of a mountain, the air's density is less, reducing atmospheric pressure.

The Earth only manages to keep its atmosphere because it is relatively large. If it were smaller its gravity pull would not be strong enough to attract the gases of the atmosphere. This has happened to the moon, where explorers have to wear weighted boots to keep their bodies down.

How big are the sun, Earth and moon?

The sun, which lies at the centre of our solar system, is about 1,390,000 kilometres (865,000 miles) in diameter. It is roughly 109 times the size of the Earth, which measures 12,757 kilometres (about 8,000 miles) across; and the Earth and the sun are on average 150,000,000 kilometres (93,000,000 miles) apart. The moon is smaller again, with a diameter of 3,456 kilometres (2,160 miles). It is 384,400 kilometres (238,857 miles) from the Earth.

What causes an eclipse of the sun?

The moon. It happens when the moon comes between the Earth and the sun so that the moon's shadow sweeps over the face of the Earth. There are two parts or depths of this shadow: the 'umbra', or total shadow, is a cone of shade where no direct sunlight penetrates; it is surrounded by the 'penumbra' or half-shadow, where there is some light.

Someone watching from within the umbra sees the sun disappear completely, entirely covered by the disc of the moon. This is a total eclipse. An observer within the penumbra sees the moon's disc projected against the sun and partly overlapping it: a partial eclipse.

Since the umbra cone is narrow and may even miss the Earth's surface completely, total eclipses are rare. In ancient times men observing them used to fear that the sun had died. But partial eclipses are far more often seen. Someone in Africa or Australia or on the Indian Ocean on 23 October 1976 would see one; or in North America on 26 February 1979; or in Africa or India on 16 February 1980.

These days will particularly interest astronomers. They can only study the 'chromosphere', or atmosphere of the sun, when its central brightness is shaded by the moon. And the eclipse of other stars and planets can be useful too. It happens whenever a celestial body passes in front of another; so most stars and planets, even the moon itself, may be eclipsed.

Where does the sun go at the end of the day?

Of course it doesn't go anywhere. In relation to the Earth, it stays more or less in the same place. But the Earth rotates on its own axis, like a spinning ball in space, and since only one side can be exposed to the sun at a time, it seems to us that the sun rises in the east and sets in the west.

For convenience we say that each day is twenty-four hours long,

but the accurate 'mean' or average length of a solar day is twenty-three hours, fifty-six minutes and four seconds. That is the time it takes the Earth to make one complete turn. The mean solar year – the time it takes to go once right round the sun, spinning all the time – is 365 days, five hours, forty-eight minutes and forty-six seconds. That is why every fourth year is a 'leap' or jumping one, to let the calendar catch up.

What is the sun?

It is the star of our solar system, roughly eight light minutes or 150,000,000 kilometres (93,000,000 miles) from Earth. Classified as a G1-type dwarf star, it is a fairly ordinary one, midway between the largest and smallest, the brightest and faintest, known. But because it is relatively near to Earth, its influence on our planet's life is immeasurably strong. The next nearest star is almost three hundred thousand times as far away.

The sun's energy comes from the conversion of hydrogen to helium at a temperature of fifteen million degrees kelvin. This happens deep in the sun's core, where pressures are many thousands of millions of times that of the Earth's atmosphere at sea level, and the density is 150 times that of water. Energy is released in the core by this nuclear process and slowly works its way to the surface, where it is radiated into space. Earth intercepts only one part in over twenty million million of this enormous energy output, but it has been so constant over geologic time scales of hundreds of millions of years that complex life forms governed by cycles of day and night, by seasons and tides, have grown up. Without the sun, in fact, life on this planet would come to an end.

What is a sunspot?

Sunspots are dark patches that appear on the sun's bright surface or sphere of light. They have a dark central region, the umbra, surrounded by a lighter outer area, the penumbra, and seem to be saucer-shaped. They are in fact regions which are cooler than the rest of the sun's surface; though even within the spot the gases are at temperatures of about 3,816° centigrade (6,800° Fahrenheit). They have strong magnetic fields, but the reason for this is not yet fully understood.

The number of spots varies over what is known as the sunspot cycle, which lasts roughly eleven years. At its minimum, perhaps only fifty sunspot groups a year will be seen, but at the maximum there may be five hundred or more. However, there are variations in the general pattern and large spots can appear at any stage of the cycle. A colossal group appeared in 1947; it covered an area of about 5,210 million square kilometres (2,000 million square miles).

What are solar flares?

These are powerful eruptions of radiation on the sun that are somehow associated with sunspots. They occur very quickly and last only fifteen to twenty minutes, or, very occasionally, two hours or more. Sometimes a type of outbreak called a 'surge' will develop rapidly above a flare.

Solar flares emit intensive short-wave and corpuscular radiation. This reaches the Earth in about twenty-six hours and causes brilliant displays of aurora and magnetic storms. The short-wave radiation also affects the layers of the ionosphere in the Earth's atmosphere and causes 'fade-outs' of radio communication.

How large is our galaxy?

It is a huge star system containing our sun and roughly 100,000 million other stars; we know it as the Milky Way. It is shaped rather like a fried egg: a spherical centre surrounded by a flat disc. It measures 100,000 light years across and is about one-fifth as thick in the thickest part.

Our sun lies more or less on the edge of the egg's yolk, or about thirty thousand light years from the centre – which is near to the constellation of Sagittarius. You can get an idea of its immense size if you think of our solar system – the sun, Earth and the eight other planets – as the size of a full-stop. Then the nearest star, Proxima Centauri, would be half a kilometre (a quarter of a mile) away, and all the stars we can see with the naked eye would be within 112 kilometres (seventy miles). But the distance across the galaxy would almost equal the diameter of the Earth.

The centre of the galaxy contains old stars, with younger ones in the long curved arms that extend from it to form the 'egg white' or disc. As they whorl in space the galaxy must look like an enormous Catherine wheel. Their speed varies with their distance from the centre. The sun is actually moving through space at about 240 kilometres (150 miles) a second; but even at that speed it will take 225 million years to go right round.

How far away is the nearest galaxy to our own?

The Andromeda galaxy can just be seen without a telescope, as a dim patch of light. It is 2·2 million light years away.

How far away is the farthest galaxy?

Nobody knows yet, because as bigger and bigger telescopes are used, more and more galaxies are discovered. About a thousand million can be seen easily with the Mount Palomar 200-inch (about 500-centimetre) telescope. With that telescope can be seen galaxies up to five thousand million light years away. We believe the Earth to be only 4,500 million years old, so the light which we receive now across these immense distances must have started on its journey towards the Earth long before the planet existed!

How far away is the nearest star to us?

Apart from our own sun – which is much the nearest star – it is the very faint Proxima Centauri, which is 4·3 light years, or forty billion kilometres (twenty-five billion miles) away. Alpha Centauri and Rigil Kentaurus are the nearest that are bright enough to be seen with the naked eye. They are both about the same distance – 4·3 light years – but both in the Southern Hemisphere.

Which is the brightest star in the night sky?

Sirius A or Alpha Canis Majoris, known as the dog star. It is in the constellation Canis Major and is seen during the winter months in the Northern Hemisphere. It is 8·7 light years or eighty-three billion kilometres (fifty-two billion miles) from our solar system, twice as big as our sun and twenty-six times brighter.

What is a white dwarf star?

The first white dwarf to be discovered was the Companion of Sirius, close to the dog star; but now some 150 white dwarfs are known and it is estimated that there are five thousand million in the Milky Way system. They are stars of low intrinsic luminosity (not very bright), roughly the same size as Earth but with a mass equal to our sun's. Their average density is a hundred thousand times that of water, but some are much denser, with a core as much as a hundred million times more dense than water. This enormous density is possible because the substance of a white dwarf is completely ionized. It contains only atomic nuclei and free electrons, which in this degenerate matter are packed more closely together than the nuclei and electrons of a normal atom, for white dwarfs represent one of the final, decaying stages in the evolution of a star.

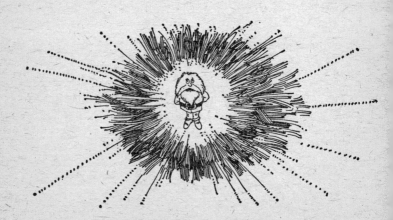

What is a 'black hole'?

No one has ever completely proved that black holes exist, but they certainly do seem to. They are claimed to exist on the basis of reason: as one of the three final stages of the evolution of a star. It is thought that when the nuclear fuel of any star whose mass is greater than that of the sun is finally burnt up, its core cools and contracts and begins to collapse under the enormous weight of the outer layers. If the mass of the star, or the energy of the matter falling in, is too great for the collapse to be halted by the formation of a white dwarf or neutron star structure, the implosion (falling in) continues indefinitely. The star has reached the black hole stage, and as a result the normal properties of space nearby are altered drastically. Everything is attracted inwards, and even light cannot escape the gravitational attraction to the centre.

What is a pulsar?

It is short for 'pulsating radio star', for these stars can only be observed on a radio telescope and they emit all their recorded radiation in the form of short regular pulses. They were first discovered in 1967 by Miss S. J. Bell.

Each pulsar keeps strictly to its own beat or pattern of pulsation, although of course the pulse rate varies from star to star. They are amazingly accurate. If the pulses were used for timekeeping, the 'clock' would be correct to a fraction of a second over the year. The pulses usually last only a few hundredths of a second and are sent out at intervals of just under a second.

Astrophysicists have not yet managed to work out a completely satisfactory theory to explain pulsars. They need to know more about the extreme physical conditions in and near the pulsars before they can do this.

What are quasars?

There are more than a hundred quasars or 'quasi-stellar radio sources' known to astronomers, but they remain objects of great mystery. They emit very strong radiation, but appear optically on photographs of the heavens as weak and small. These star-like objects must be several thousand million light years from Earth; but the energy they send out is several hundred times as intense as that of ordinary galaxies much larger in size. So theories about quasars are still being put forward, and they will probably puzzle astronomers for a long time.

How did the universe begin?

There are two theories: evolutionary and steady state.

The evolutionary theory was put forward by Georges Lemaître, who argued that about twenty thousand million years ago all the matter in the universe – enough perhaps to make a hundred thousand million galaxies – was concentrated in one small mass, which he called the 'primeval atom'. For some reason this primeval atom, which would have been of incredibly high density, exploded and sent its matter out in every direction. When the force of the explosion died down, the matter formed into galaxies; but later something provoked them to start expanding again. Other people proposed variations on this theme, but essentially all the supporters of the evolutionary theory believe that the universe was formed in one place and at one point in time and since then has been expanding.

The steady state theory proposed by Fred Hoyle, Thomas Gold and

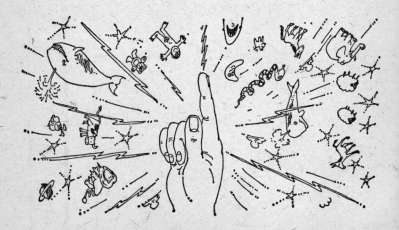

Herman Bondi maintains that the universe as a whole has always looked the same and will always do so. As the galaxies expand away from one another, new material is forced in some way between them, making up new galaxies to replace those that have receded. So the general distribution of galaxies remains the same.

Other theories are being developed all the time; we may never know the complete answer.

Where did the Earth come from?

This question has been asked by astronomers throughout the ages. One theory was put forward by the French mathematician, Laplace, who lived from 1749 to 1827. It was called the 'nebular hypothesis'. Laplace supposed that the sun was formed by a gas cloud which, as it contracted and grew hotter, began to rotate at high speed. The sun then began to bulge at its equator until finally it threw off a ring of material. This happened several times, and eventually the rings of matter condensed to make the planets of the solar system. However, it has since been shown that rings like this – even if they could be formed – would not condense in this way.

In the early part of this century, Sir James Jeans suggested that early in the sun's history another star passed close by, and the gravitational interaction between that star and the sun drew a cigar-shaped filament of matter from the sun. As the star receded it set this matter in motion around the sun, and eventually the material condensed to form the Earth and the other planets. But this theory was found to be mathematically unsound and was abandoned also.

Recently there has been a swing back towards Laplace's nebular hypothesis, and several theories have been proposed that are based on its general theme. If we suppose that the sun was surrounded by a cloud of gas and dust, this material would eventually settle into a disc. Irregularities would cause accretion; that is, lumps would start to form. Large lumps would tend to attract other pieces of matter, and in this way the planets might have gradually condensed.

But really we have no completely satisfactory answer to the question – Where *did* the Earth come from?

Will the world ever come to an end?

Yes, if astronomers are right in their prediction about the sun. It is quite a small dwarf star and only seems bright and powerful because it is relatively near the Earth. But calculations on evolutionary models forecast that eventually the sun will become a red giant. It will happen when all its hydrogen is burned up, and nuclear reactions involving helium and heavier atoms take over. The sun's chemical composition will change. It will increase in size and luminosity and probably engulf the Earth.

When all the nuclear energy sources are used up, the sun will reach its last stage. Its radius will shrink to roughly one-hundredth of its present size, and it will become a white dwarf. Over many billions of years its internal temperature and its brightness will gradually decrease until it finishes as a black dwarf, a very dense, non-luminous object of degenerate matter.

But there is no need to worry! No one can predict the lifetime of the sun accurately, but it is estimated at approximately ten thousand million years.

What is a comet?

It is a celestial body made of gas and small particles, with large solid particles in the star-like nucleus. The particles are mainly ice. Comets vary in size but an average diameter is about 128 thousand kilometres (eighty thousand miles) with the nucleus very much smaller and the tail perhaps millions of kilometres long. They are very tenuous and hardly disturb the orbits of planets as they pass. They travel in elongated ellipses, almost parabolic in shape, at speeds varying from 1,100 kilometres (700 miles) per hour in outer space to about two million kilometres (one and a quarter million miles) per hour when they are near the sun.

When a comet is far away from the sun, it possesses no visible tail and looks like a faint fuzzy smudge. But as it comes closer to the sun the ice and other materials begin to melt and give off gases which form the 'coma' surrounding the nucleus. Pressure of radiation from the sun drives the tiny comet particles out into space, and this causes the tail, which, because of the radiation pressure, always points away from the sun. So comets lose part of their mass each time they pass close to the sun. This is why short-period comets are usually very faint, while the bright ones are seen very infrequently. And comet periods vary enormously, from Encke's comet every three-and-a-third years to the longest, in the region of a million years or more. We know that approximately three hundred approach the sun every century and so, making allowance for undetected ones, there are probably as many as 120,000 in the whole solar system. Halley's comet, named after the eighteenth-century astronomer, is the brightest that has a relatively short period. It is seen roughly every seventy-five years.

Because comets are so striking in appearance, they were often recorded in ancient annals: perhaps as forewarnings of some disastrous event such as war, plague or famine. They were noticed particularly by the Chinese, who called them 'besom stars', because the tail looks a little like the traditional witch's broom. The earliest mentions go back to the seventh century BC, and these references can be very useful in historical research. If modern astronomers are able to identify the comet described, the sighting may be used to put a precise date to a particular historical event.

What are Saturn's rings?

Saturn is the sixth major planet and is 1,417,000,000 kilometres (885,900,000 miles) from the sun. Its unique system of surrounding rings was first noticed by Galileo in 1610, but with his tiny telescope he could not see clearly what they were. Then in 1665 the Dutch astronomer Huygens was able to identify them.

The outer diameter of the ring system is about 274,000 kilometres (171,000 miles), while the inner diameter is 149,000 kilometres (93,000 miles); and they are between eleven and twenty-four kilometres (seven and fifteen miles) thick.

They cannot be solid or liquid sheets, for they lie within the area of space in which a solid ring would be disrupted by the planet's powerful gravity. Besides, it was established by J. E. Keeler in 1895 that the inner section rotates more rapidly than the outer parts. So the whole system must consist of swarms of particles that are too small to be seen independently. No one knows for sure what these particles are made of, but their high 'albedo' (reflecting power) and the negligible mass of the ring system indicate that they are made of ice. They may be debris from an old satellite of Saturn that approached the planet too closely and was broken up.

Why do stars shine?

The nearest 'star' we can see well is our own sun, 150 million kilometres (ninety-three million miles) from Earth. The temperature ranges from 6,000° kelvin at its surface to 20,000,000° kelvin at its core as helium is formed by the fusion of hydrogen nuclei.

The stars of the night sky are suns as well. They seem small only because they are millions of miles away. In fact those visible to the naked eye vary in size from about the diameter of the Earth to as much as 250 times larger than our sun. Their brightness depends on their mass and size, and with binoculars or a telescope it is possible to distinguish between the very bright ones farther away from us, and those less bright but closer.

Why does the moon shine?

It is light from the sun, reflected from the moon's surface; and as the moon changes its position in relation to the sun, more or less of the sunlit portion can be seen.

At full moon, the moon is placed directly opposite the sun with the Earth in between; so the whole face of the moon is visible to us. When the moon is 'new' and 'old', only a crescent section catches the sun's rays, because the moon is lying between us and the sun.

Is there a man on the moon?

Apart from astronauts, no! But the mountains and dry seas of the moon do sometimes seem to make a face. And we can see them so clearly because the moon has hardly any atmosphere.

We have sunshine, moonshine and starshine: is there Earthshine?

Yes there is, and you can see it quite clearly when the moon is new or old. At night, the sun's light reflects from the Earth on to the moon in just the same way as it reflects from the moon to make moonlight for us. Since the phases of the Earth and moon are complementary, Earthshine is strongest when the moon is not full. So, beside the moon's crescent there is a shadowy disc – the rest of the moon illuminated by light reflected from the surface of the Earth.

Why aren't we bombarded with meteorites?

We are! At least, the Earth is bombarded from space by meteors or shooting stars. These are small particles that enter the Earth's atmosphere at high speeds of about seventy-two kilometres (forty-five miles) per second: that is, 256,000 kilometres (160,000 miles) per hour. As it plunges through the atmosphere, the particle is heated to incandescence. Atoms escape, and collide with molecules of air to form a bright streak in the sky along the meteor's path. Harvard Observatory has estimated that over 100,000 million meteors penetrate our atmosphere every twenty-four hours.

But only between one and thirty of these fireballs of metal or stone actually fall to Earth during a twenty-four-hour period. This is because most of them disintegrate and burn high up. And since much of the Earth's surface is covered with water many that do penetrate the atmosphere fail to strike land.

The largest known meteorite was found in 1920 at Holoa West near Grootfontein in South-West Africa; it weighed about sixty tonnes. Forty miles north of Vanavara, in Siberia, at just after midnight on 30 June 1908, there was a huge explosion which devastated an area of about 3,840 square kilometres (1,500 square miles). The shockwave was felt 950 kilometres (600 miles) away. This explosion has been put down to a giant meteorite hitting the Earth.

At Deep Bay, Saskatchewan, there is a great gash 13·6 kilometres (8·5 miles) across that was probably caused by a meteorite; and the hole ninety-five kilometres wide and 394 metres deep (sixty miles by 1,300 feet) in the basin of the River Popigai in Russia has the same origin. But the largest proven meteorite crater is Coon Butte, near Canyon Diablo at Winslow, Arizona. It is 1,265 metres (4,150 feet) in diameter and about 175 metres (575 feet) deep. Scientists who discovered the crater in 1891 estimated that an iron nickel mass about seventy-six metres (250 feet) wide and weighing two million tonnes must have gouged it out some twenty-seven thousand years ago.

The largest meteorite to fall in the United Kingdom exploded over Coventry on Christmas Eve 1965. Forty-one kilogrammes (ninety pounds) of stony material was picked up near Barwell in Leicestershire. The largest piece weighed about eight kilogrammes (eighteen pounds).

Is there life on other planets?

The answer is probably yes. There are millions of stars like our own sun throughout the universe, so the chances of there being another planetary system capable of supporting life is high. Certainly, there are enough of the basic elements that make up the structures of life if only the conditions are right.

And remember, too, that life out there in the universe would not necessarily be similar to what we know on Earth. The physical and mental processes of living creatures in another world could be so different to our own that we would not recognize them.